SEEKING GOD'S PROMISES
THROUGH TIMES OF TRIALS

COUNT IT ALL
joy

KIMBERLY LECAR

"Count It All Joy!" Seeking God's Promises Through Times of Trials. Copyright © 2025 Crowned In Beauty LLC
All rights reserved.

All rights reserved. No part of this publication may be reproduced, distributed and or transmitted without any written permission by the author or publisher. This includes photocopying, recording or any electronic or mechanical methods except in the case of brief quotations for the purposes of reviews or other noncommercial uses permitted by copyright law. For permissions see address below.

"Count It All Joy! Seeking God's Promises through Times of Trials" is a Bible Study based on names, characters, and places of the Bible, in which the author has been inspired by and shares life experiences and applications for encouragement. All personal experiences shared throughout this work is not a substitution to any professional therapy, counseling and does not substitute the Word of God.

Scripture quotations taken from The Holy Bible, New International Version®, NIV®. Copyright © 1973, 1978, 1984, 2011 by Biblica, Inc. Used with permission of Zondervan. All rights reserved worldwide. www.zondervan.com This publication has adopted commentaries and used the resources to enhance the understanding of theological, cultural concepts.(See Endnotes)

Printed in the United States of America

ISBN: 978-1-7378091-3-5 (paperback)

For permissions request, address "Attention: Permissions Coordinator"
Crowned In Beauty, LLC
PSC 427 BOX 1966
APO, AE 09630

Photography by C. Miracle Photographey LLC
Cover, Book Design & Graphic Design used under Canva Pro License by Kimberly Lecar
at www.crownedinbeauty.com

CONTENTS

ACKNOWLEDGEMENTS	4
FORWARD	6
TESTIMONIALS	9
ABOUT THE AUTHOR	11
A LETTER	12
HOW TO USE THIS STUDY	13
WEEK 1 *THE PROMISES & CHARACTER OF GOD*	16
WEEK 2 *THE FATHER OF NATIONS: ABRAHAM*	49
WEEK 3 *LONGING, WAITING & SURRENDER: HANNAH*	83
WEEK 4 *THE RIGHTEOUS SERVANTS: ELIZABETH & ZECHARIAH*	114
WEEK 5 *FULFILLMENT OF THE PROMISE OF JOY: MARY & JOSEPH*	144
TREASURE CHEST	177
NAMES OF GOD	179
REFERENCE VERSES	180
ENDNOTES	181
ABOUT CROWNED IN BEAUTY	182
BOOKS	183
ABOUT FOUNTAINS OF HOPE	184

www.crownedinbeauty.com

This Bible Study is dedicated to **Brenda Parker of Fountains of Hope Counseling** in Sierra Vista, Arizona; who taught me how to seek the heart of God and to continue seeking a life of un-offense. To count my trials as God's graces. Your love and your wisdom will continue to serve as a guide in my journey of healing. God knew the exact time He would send me on the final chapter of those darkest days. He sent me to the desert, to the Light of Christ within you, where you guided me. Your humility and love for Christ gave me permission to embrace that I am Crowned in Beauty.

In memory of My Tia Millie. You fought the good fight until the end. Even in your pain you reminded me to be grateful for what I have. You loved me like a mother, because truly I was blessed to have you as my mother's sister. I miss hearing your laugh and the way you danced through life, now you are living in that Joy with King Jesus.

In memory of Tisha. You fought the good fight and taught me to run hard after Jesus. I remember the first day I met you and how you held my hand. I saw Jesus in you. You always encouraged me and said "that is what we are called to do as Brothers and Sisters in Christ." I am forever grateful for the way you exemplified a life of Joy because of God's love for us. I miss you.

With Love, to my husband who through our own trials humbled himself and saw a woman who needed healing and still does. Yet you continue to choose to run this race with me.

Elias, the day the Lord opens your mouth you will prophesy of His great wonders.

My Mother, who opened her heart to simply listen to my experiences and began the walk of forgiveness long before this study came to be. My Father's Ruben and Robert, I love you. My Brother, I am so proud of the man you have become. To Daisy and Amber, I love you more than words could describe. To my nieces and nephews,
I trust the Lord will do great things through you.

With adoration to Denise, Kayla, Linda, Rebekah, Cece and Esther. Your prayers and friendship have held my arms up. You have seen me at my worst and continue to love me.

Thank you to my Team of Beta Readers who wholeheartedly made time to go through this study and made themselves available to be a part of the CIB ministry.
Your thoughtful insight will be carried through each page.

With appreciation to all the women that have allowed me to speak into their lives and to walk this road together, Lamm, Danielle, Anna C, Lindsey, Sarah W, Sarah H, Terri, Heather D, Cherie M.

With appreciation to Jill Hatchett of F.A.S.T. GIRL INC and Danitza Mack of DMAC Consulting Group LLC, you both bring out the GOLD and your grace
and love hold a special place in my heart.

My Lord, Savior Jesus Christ who continues to extend His grace over my life. One day I will stand before the throne and put on the crown of life that awaits me to worship you in eternity. You continue to show me what a grace-filled life is as you replaced the ashes of my past for beauty.

Forward by Dr. Richelle Clark

Dear Sister,

Sometimes things in life do not go as we hope. We may experience great pain and disappointment from divorce, health challenges, infertility, and financial woes. Perhaps we have a hard time accepting that life isn't fair and we become angry, sad or even defeated. But we are not alone in our pain. God is with us. He can replace our disappointment with joy — no matter what is going on in our lives. Just think of joy as a road map leading us away from a dark path. Joy is also the light allowing us to better see the road ahead. I am so glad Kimberly Lecar wrote about joy and uses this bible study to remind us that God is stronger than our disappointments.

I have known Kimberly for more than a decade. We met at a women's bible study in Germany, and bonded over our love of God, running and journalism. Kimberly is the literal voice of my audio book, "Running for your life! A devotional for women to run slow, walk fast or jog with reckless abandon." She was my training partner when we ran a half-marathon in Mainz, Germany. And Kimberly continues to offer me words of encouragement and reminds me about the unmovable, loving force that is God. If you are reading this book, you too will get to know Kimberly, hear about her faith walk and how she hopes to help you find joy.

Kimberly has lead women's bible studies and worked in Christian leadership roles at U.S. military churches in the United States and Europe. She is a loving wife and mom, and Christian singer/songwriter. She often speaks to groups about her faith and inspiring life story. She lives her faith daily and is not afraid to share her love of God with anyone who wants to listen.

What I most enjoy about her book is it prompts us to read the word of God to get to know Him. I like to think of this study as a relationship book because we are learning to have a relationship with God. We are getting to know him and his character, and in doing so, we are sharpening our own character.

I have watched Kimberly be refined by life's challenges and emerge with joy — a joy that caused her to share her story to inspire other women to get closer to God and find joy. I too have been refined by life's fiery trials and I am grateful for friends like Kimberly, who encourage me in my faith and gently nudge me toward God when I am tempted to handle things on my own. This study also reminds us to trust God and find our worth and value not in this world, but in Him. Kimberly writes that we are who God says we are: We are the children of God!

As I read through this study, I am also reminded of my favorite Psalm — 138. I learned it with the title God Answered My Prayer. The King James version writes, "In the day when I cried, thou answered me and strengthened me with strength in my soul." This passage reminds me that joy is also God's strength. We can lean on God to get through tough times and this process strengthens us and draws us closer to Him.

This Bible study is easy to follow but it requires courage. You must let go of the things that have burdened you to embrace God's joy. You have to be willing to get to know God and His character so that you can more easily find joy. It is my hope this bible study will change your spiritual life. Sister, you are worthy of God's joy!

With joy in Christ,
Dr. Richelle Larice Clark
Historian and Author

TESTIMONIALS

"Count It All Joy!" is a beautiful reminder that God is a God of promises. He is a promise keeper! He is always with us in times of trial, and He is a redeemer! What the enemy means for evil He turns to good! I loved diving into scripture and the reminders of where God has been in the midst of everything. He is the same God yesterday, today, and forever! - **Mary Andrews, Texas**

It has been such an honor to do life with my friend & author Kimberly Lecar since 2017. We have walked each other through some real life accountability that has now led us to living lives of true freedom. This Bible study, is the result of her hard work and desire to hear from God through his word. It is possible to live a life surrendered, disciplined and full of joy after regularly spending time reading Gods word. It is truth and it transforms us. Kimberly intentionally uses these chapters to teach you more about the heart of God and his role in the lives of several important biblical characters. Her real life testimony is also sprinkled throughout and I applaud her for courageously adding that to this Bible study. The word of God in the book of Revelation says we overcome by the blood of the lamb and the word of our testimony. She is modeling that for us within these pages. May we all learn to renew our minds through studying scripture from a Bible study like this one. This is an exciting time people are returning to church and desiring to read the truth found in Gods word. It is life giving. I hope you will enjoy the stories and truths found among the pages of this Bible study and learn to live a life of joy trusting in God every day.

-Denise Keeter, Freedom Through His Word Ministries, Alabama

TESTIMONIALS

It was a joy to complete this Bible Study. I loved how this study was written in such a personal way, it was so encouraging and it left me not wanting to finish the last day because I didn't want it to be over. Whether you are a new Christian or strong in your faith, I am sure you will learn more about the character and love of God and how with Him, we can count it all joy. **-LeAndra Smith, North Carolina**

I remember when I first saw Kimberly at a PWOC meeting in Germany. I was new in my faith during that time and I saw the ladies praying over Kimberly since she was moving to England for their next duty station. Little did I know that I would be moving to England a couple of months later and quickly learned how God is always preparing the way for you-in this case, for Kimberly and I to meet in England and form a beautiful friendship that has continued through different time zones and different continents. She is a prayer warrior and her love for the Lord is evident in the way that she speaks and lives her life. She has been the most encouraging friend that has helped me deepen my faith so when I started her Bible study, I had tears of joy because it was like I was physically sitting next to my friend again, hearing her encouraging words keeping our eyes and mind focused on who the Lord is. Count it All Joy gives us a time to reflect on where our hearts are and reminds us who God is and the promises that He keeps, that no matter what we are going through, we can "Count it All Joy!" — **Lamphanh Huettner, Connecticut**

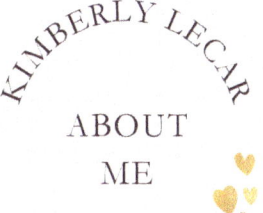

KIMBERLY LECAR
ABOUT ME

Hi friend!

I am blessed and privileged that you have allowed me to tag along with you on this journey of life! A little bit about me.

I am a wife of an Army Soldier, Mother of Elias, Author, Speaker, Singer-Songwriter, and Artist. After writing my first devotional "Crowned in Beauty: A devotional of songs and the testimonies that inspired them" in 2019, I founded the ministry which is now known as, Crowned In Beauty. It is a haven for women seeking healing from life's trials. My own journey—marked by triumph over trauma—fuels me with passion to help others find beauty in the ashes of everyday life.

Favorite Beverage: Coffee and Water
Favorite Places to Visit: London, Madrid, Köln, Rome
Favorite Songs: How Great Thou Art & I Can Only Imagine, Holy Forever
Life Verse: Matthew 6:33

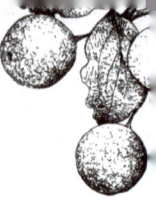

He Loves You Dearly

Beloved,

God is who He says he is, and I am honored that he chose us for such a time as this. It's hard to put into words the love I have found in Christ. The faith I have grown into and the cost of Jesus on the cross from where I was and where I am today has been filled with unsurmountable blessings, lessons and moments of joy. As I write this letter, I reflect on a life of almost 17 years in which I have seen the miracles, healings, deliverance and freedom through the salvation of The Lord.

In 2019 my husband and I embarked on an adventure called IVF (in-vitro fertilization). It happened to be the year that prior to going through treatment, the Lord impressed the title of this study on my heart. With time I began to understand that God was calling me into a deeper relationship with Him through a whirlwind of surrender and countless encounters of dealing with unbelief, doubt, and longing for healing from past trauma.

I have learned and am still learning what a life of surrender to Christ means and how to 'Count it All Joy.' Through perseverance my faith has been built and continues to be rooted and establish in Him. As we journey together for the next 5 weeks my prayer is that you would see the promises of God to which He has called you into a life of surrender, trust and obedience. Through it I believe that in the end you will 'Count It All Joy' because of our loving Lord and Savior, Jesus Christ.

You ARE Crowned in Beauty,
Kimberly

How to use this study

This 5 Week Bible Study is split into 5 study days. While it may take around 30 minutes for each heart-work lesson, I encourage you to take your time with each reflection* and let the Word of God reveal itself to you. Some days may require more reading times than others. For those who like to put pen to paper, I have provided blank note-taking pages before and after each day.

The icons below will be spread throughout the study. Use them as an opportunity and guide to dig deeper into the Word!

God's Character	Bible Reading	Author's Testimony
Collecting Your Treasure	Application	Reflection
Searching with intention	Guidance	Take time to Pray

*The sections for reflection are based off of my personal experiences and what has helped me grow throughout my inner healing journey. These sections are by no means meant to be replaced by any professional counseling and are an extension of my understanding in specific areas of psychology and truama response. I encourage you to seek professionals and to use this study to help you grow deeper in your faith and above all that it bring you closer to God. *

NOTES

NOTES

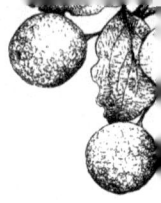

WEEK 1

The Promises & Character of God

WEEK 1: DAY 1

<u>The God of Promises</u>

Where are you today? Are you in the secret place before the presence of God?

Or have you found yourself wandering into comparison land, thinking,

Life would be better if _____ (fill in the blank),

then my purpose...

Friend, you are not alone. There are times when God's no is not now. If you look through the Bible, you'll see countless stories of people who waited decades for "it" to come to pass. Some never saw "it" come to pass but their faith helped them persevere through life's challenges. I have learned that pushing against Gods will, is partnered with built in resistance.

In Genesis 3:9, after the foundations of the earth were formed, God made Adam in His image and Eve from Adam's rib. But after Eve was deceived and ate from the tree of knowledge *[Note: the tree of Knowledge]* she also gave it to Adam to eat.

Then we read **Genesis 3:8-10**

8 "The Lord God, as He was walking in the garden in the cool of the day, heard the man and his wife hide. 9 But the Lord God called to the man, 'Where are you?' 10 He answered, 'I heard you in the garden, and I was afraid because I was naked, so I hid.'"

WEEK 1: DAY 1

They hid. Shame, guilt, disappointment and fear—all these feelings made them hide. These emotions can influence us to hide too, causing us to isolate ourselves.

When we lack accountability, our growing faith is hindered. I believe that when you are a child of God, not having genuine accountability from God-fearing, loving people can prevent the necessary character refinement for becoming more like Christ.

Our character is a reflection of our beliefs and values.

I can say with certainty that in the past, my beliefs and values didn't always align with my character.

But where does our character come from?

What does that even mean, and why are we about to study "character"?

- Your character is shaped by your will, your understanding of yourself, and how you portray yourself to the world.
- You can develop the traits your character may lack through time and consistency.

Now, imagine you have a goal and at your core, you truly believe it will happen. Regardless of your circumstances, your character will either prove or disprove your commitment to that goal. Character is defined as the qualities that describe how a person acts, feels, and thinks. These traits are often shaped early in life and through self-reflection and intentionality, we can grow in refining them.

WEEK 1: DAY 1

In 2008, I surrendered my life to Christ, declaring Jesus as my Savior and Lord. It was a cool Monday night, I was on my knees at the beach, having just rid myself of paraphernalia used for witchcraft. I cried out to God desperate for meaning, love, purpose, and peace. I was living a life that acknowledged Jesus but didn't understand what it meant to surrender.

My faith was based on family tradition.

If you have asked yourself what my personal goal may be, friend my goal is not a tangible one. Although this Bible study is a by-product of it, my goal is to continue to glorify God through each difficulty and moments of joy for His purposes. However that looks, painting, writing, sitting, serving, loving, or listening, my goal: eternal life with Our Father. Before we move forward on this treasure hunt as I will call it so we can **'Count it All Joy!'** through God's promises, I have a question that I would like you to consider.

Where are you? Where is your heart today in terms of forgiveness, hurt, shame, guilt, anger, disappointment, or doubt? Being vulnerable is hard, trust me I know.

The reward, Jesus, is greater.

Take a moment to write your answer below.
When we address what may be hindering us, or why we feel stuck, or life is not where *I* wanted it to be, the cost of surrender equals kingdom income.

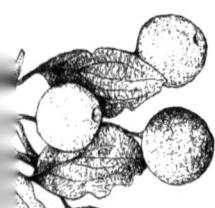

WEEK 1: DAY 1

Let's examine and reconcile our hearts with Christ, beginning with repentance. If you haven't fully surrendered your life to Christ yet, why not take that step today?

<u>For Your Heart</u>

God, you who made the foundations of the earth, whose Spirit hovered over the waters and made man in your likeness, I come to you today, knowing that my life and joy, depend on my complete surrender to you. I ask for your forgiveness for holding on to beliefs such as

_____

(e.g., I'm not worthy, I'll never have a spouse, I am ugly).

Lord, you sent Jesus to die on my behalf and on that cross, everything I've done or believed that is contrary to you was nailed there and forgiven. Today, I declare that by the blood of Christ, I am forgiven, redeemed, and I seek to do your will. I desire to abide in you, to seek you daily for your purposes. In Jesus' name, Amen.

Whether you've just accepted Jesus today or have been walking with Him for years, know this: You are who He says you are, Chosen. Loved. Forgiven. Adopted and more! As a reminder throughout this study, why not take some time to write these treasures in your treasure box, found on page 178, and continue to live a life that honors the Lord.

WEEK 1: DAY 1

John 15:2: *"He prunes every branch in Me that does not bear good fruit."*

God desires for you to be in His will and to delight in Him. When you do, you will reap a harvest of blessings and show to others the 'good fruit.' Most importantly, it's all for His glory. We will see shortly as he told Abram, "I am your reward." (Genesis 15:1). As children of God, we possess that reward—if we choose to take it. But, we must keep Him at the center of all things.

Our time studying who God is, learning more about his character and applying his word to our lives builds and establishes our faith.

Before we begin our journey together with Abraham, Sarah, Hannah, Elkanah, Elizabeth, Mary, Joseph and Jesus, we will focus our attention on studying the character of God and His promises. I too will share parts of my journey and lessons throughout. I'm here with you friend and we are treasure hunting together. I pray that you reflect on today's study and begin living a life that truly, "Counts It All Joy!"

You are Crowned in Beauty,

Kimberly

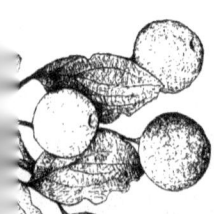

NOTES

WEEK 1: DAY 2

El Elyon: The Character of God

Blessed Be! Praise Be! Welcome to a New Day of Discoveries!

Let's begin by reading **Genesis 14:14-20**

After recovering his family members and their possessions, we read that Melchizedek, the King of Salem, meets Abram with bread and wine and blesses him, saying:

"Blessed be Abram by God Most High,
Creator of Heaven and Earth,
20 and praise be to God Most High,
Who delivered your enemies into your hand."
Then Abram gave him a tenth of everything.

Take a moment to write out what **'God Most High"** means and what it reveals about who God is. In this moment of your life what is one word that speaks to you about who God is. What would it be and why?

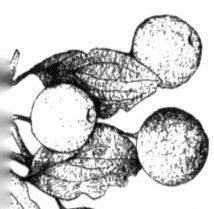

WEEK 1: DAY 2

Growing up in the Catholic faith, I viewed God as an unapproachable, God of wrath. Between the ages of 9 and 14, I remember standing in front of altars in our home filled with pictures of saints and some deceased family members. However, after experiencing sexual abuse, my time spent in prayer dwindled, and I began to question God's existence.

God is who He says He is.

When the Lord reveals himself to us, we should continually trust in Him. With time I have come to understand that the faster I run to Him the more at peace I am. When we look around at the world today we may ask ourselves, "Why all the turmoil?"
While my belief in God remained, my reverence for His word and my longing for understanding faded. I was left with many questions like,
"Why did this happen?" "How could God allow this?"

If you have experienced setbacks, traumas, or challenges at any point in your life, have you asked God about the purpose for them?

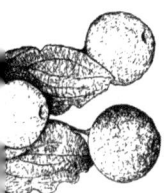

WEEK 1: DAY 2

Let's return to **Genesis 14** for a moment. This chapter speaks of a war between four kings and five others. The four kings end up conquering the Amalekites and Amorites. We learn that the five kings instigated the war, only to lose. In the midst of this, Lot (Abram's nephew) and his family are captured along with the plunder. This prompts Abram to gather 318 select men, form an army, and pursue the enemy kings. After a successful rescue mission, Abram recovers his family.

Then, we are introduced to Melchizedek, the priest, who witnesses Abram honoring the Lord by giving a tenth of his possessions. In this chapter, we find one of the many characteristics of God.

Fill in the blanks below:

"Blessed be Abram by _____ _____, and _____ _____ _____.

And praise be to _____ _____ _____ who delivered your enemies into your hand."

God is Most High.
God is the Creator of Heaven and Earth.
God is to be praised.
God is the Deliverer.

WEEK 1: DAY 2

Amidst the chaos in the world God remains, worthy of praise. He created the heavens and the earth and everything in it. He delivered Lot, using Abram as His willing vessel.

In the years following the abuse, I struggled to understand how or why anyone would praise and worship God after experiencing trauma. Slowly, I became numb to the world around me. I lived in a constant state of anxiety, low self-esteem, feelings of unworthiness, grief, and anger. At times, rage seemed to consume me, spilling into other areas of my life.

Sadly, I began to accept the lie that what happened to me was deserved. I felt dirty, unlovable, and convinced that people like me; people who have been abused were treated that way because of what happened to them. Yet, deep within me, I knew there was more to my story. I needed to trust, get grounded in my faith, and move forward. Most importantly, I needed to choose to forgive. For about 30 years of my life, I admit I extended forgiveness to certain people and with conditions.

Today, I am able to search for areas of my life where I see that Jesus was present. It's like finding gold! I see it more each day but it wasn't an easy journey.
I am learning to 'Count It All Joy!' each day.

WEEK 1: DAY 2

Sometimes, we fail to see treasures in the "in-between" seasons of life.

Is there any 'gold' you can write about today? Places, situations and people where you see Jo?

Finish todays' lesson by reading **John 1:1-5**

Remember the light shines in the darkness, and every day there is hope and freedom—in Christ.

God brought your 'Melchizedek'—that shining light,

the High Priest Jesus Christ—into your life. If you take a moment to search your heart,

I'm sure the answer will be clear. He loves you dearly.

You are Crowned in Beauty,

Kimberly

NOTES

WEEK 1: DAY 3

El Shaddai & El Roi
"The Sovereign God & The God Who Sees"

Yesterday, we explored the first of many of God's character traits: *El Elyon, God Most High*. As we continue on this journey, I encourage you to keep searching for God's character and attributes long after you've completed this study. There is so much more to Him than we can cover here. We're just laying the foundation for what's to come in the weeks ahead.

God Appears to Abram.

After Melchizedek blesses the Lord, God appears to Abram in a vision saying,

"Do not be afraid, Abram, I am your shield, your very great reward."

El Elyon appears to Abram as a shield. Not a literal shield like the one soldiers carried, but in a spiritual sense. Let's camp out here for a moment.

We have learned much about the specific charter of God as *El Elyon*, why do you think God tells Abram that He is his shield and reward?

What do you think The Lord is alluding to about Abram's character?

WEEK 1: DAY 3

But Abram responds: "*Sovereign Lord*, what can you give me since I remain childless, and the one who will inherit my estate is Eliezer of Damascus?"

Abram calls God "*Sovereign*." Why does he do this?

The word "sovereign" has several meanings. First, it means having supreme power or authority. It also refers to a king or queen as the head of a monarchy, ruling over a people or government. Yet, when we examine the word "sovereign" through a biblical lens, we see that God's power, authority, and control are extended over everything.

Let's read about it.

Read Genesis 15:2

As we read on, we see that Abram acknowledges the right to an offspring comes from God. At that point, Abram was childless, and he thought his servant, Eliezer, would inherit his estate.

Now read Read Genesis 15:3-8

What do you notice in these passages about what God says about Himself?

WEEK 1: DAY 3

God begins by telling Abram who He is: "I am the Lord, who brought you out of Ur of the Chaldeans." He is personal, reminding Abram of what He has already done for him and what He will give him. And Abram responds again, calling God "*Sovereign Lord*," seeking reassurance on how he will possess the land.

Have you ever felt like you had to prove yourself—like prove your character or integrity to others? How did that feel?

God patiently answers Abram's questions.

In 2018, I had the privilege of living in England, and I recall as a child my mother tuning into the television to watch the wedding of Prince Charles and the late Princess Diana. The long train of Princess Diana's dress filling the entrance of Saint Paul's Cathedral, the puffy shoulders on her dress, the guards, the jewels, and the horse-drawn carriage—Cinderella's wedding couldn't compare to the grandeur of what I was witnessing.

When I visited The Crown Jewels in London, I learned about the late Queen Elizabeth II and the significance of bowing or curtseying to a sovereign. I reflected on the significance of a bow or curtsy. It was and is a sign of reverence.

WEEK 1: DAY 3

The word for that season of my life was: *Sovereign.*

Living in England with my husband provided us many opportunities. While I was enjoying the adventure of traveling the world, deep inside, I felt like God let us remain childless in our marriage for many reasons. I remember asking my friends, "How can a Sovereign God, who knows my heart and gave me this desire, not allow me to conceive naturally?" I wrestled with the idea of undergoing IVF (in-vitro fertilization). I feared that if I proceeded, I would be interfering with God's plan for my family. Over time, I realized that I was dealing with unbelief. I repented and decided to trust God, regardless of the outcome,

and began the IVF journey.

Let's return to **Genesis 16**. Here we meet Sarai, Abram's wife, who has been childless. She becomes impatient and urges Abram to have a child with her servant, Hagar.

Read Genesis 16.

Hagar, after conceiving, faces pain and embarrassment, and she flees. But the angel of the Lord appears to her, asking about her whereabouts, and offers her encouragement and a blessing in the midst of her pain. Hagar then praises the Lord.

Genesis 16:13

She gave this name to the Lord who spoke to her: "You are the God who sees me," for she said, "I have now seen the One who sees me."

WEEK 1: DAY 3

Sometimes our situations lead us to places of isolation. Abiding in the stillness of God is often challenging. Our flesh wants what it wants, but now. The stillness I am referring to is God's constant peace, and with it comes His glory. When was the last time you were "still" and felt the glory of the Lord? That tangible weight that your "knower" knows you are standing before *"El Roi."* Take a moment to reflect.

Looking at real encounters with God in His Word helps us build our faith. Most importantly, it reveals God's heart for His people. He is a God of covenant promises. After the birth of Ishmael, Hagar's son, we read that the Lord appears to Abram 11 years later saying:

"I am God Almighty. Live in my presence and be blameless. I will set up my covenant between me and you, and I will multiply you greatly."

Then Abram fell prostrate to worship the God who spoke to him.

Reflect on how personal God is with you. Do you see Him in the intimate details of your life? When He speaks to your heart, what has He impressed upon you?

WEEK 1: DAY 3

Genesis 17:1 says: **"I am God Almighty."** **El Shaddai, the All-Sufficient One.**
In Hebrew, the root of this word means "breast" or "mountain,"
signifying both nourishment and strength.

As you reflect on where you are today, take a moment to consider how God has provided for humanity through the ages. The all-sufficient God who sees, who is sovereign, who is all-knowing, says: "I am the Lord God Almighty." Through Christ, He provided—and like He told Abraham to "walk with me blameless," our obedience to Him is key. There is so much more to learn about God. We've only scratched the surface.

Today, I encourage you to take account of how you are living your life. May it be lived in a way that produces endurance, so that you may be complete in Christ, lacking nothing. Remember to turn to God for wisdom in each season of your life,
as **James 1:3-5** encourages us to do.

You are Crowned in Beauty,
Kimberly

NOTES

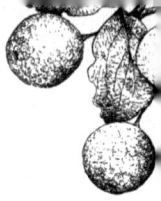

WEEK 1: DAY 4

A Blessed Promise

"Blessed is the one who perseveres under trials, because, having stood the test, that person will receive the crown of life that the Lord has promised to those who love Him." James 1:12

There are so many treasures that await us in the coming weeks as we reflect on **James 1:12.** Have you considered what a joyous day it will be when you receive your crown of life? What does this verse tell you about what God desires for you? Reflect on the verses below 'looking intently' to words the Lord is highlighting. Use the space below and make sure to add them to the treasure box on page 178.

Psalm 119:41

May Your unfailing love come to me, Lord, Your salvation, according to Your promise.

2 Peter 3:9

The Lord is not slow in keeping His promise, as some understand slowness. Instead, He is patient with you, not wanting anyone to perish, but everyone to come to repentance.

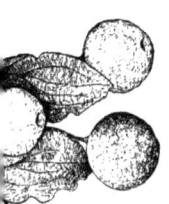

WEEK 1: DAY 4

We've been given another day—a day we can't take for granted. We have no idea what tomorrow holds let alone the next five minutes. As you've been taking inventory of your character and emotions, what has God revealed to you? In all things, God remains faithful. He blesses and gives the crown of life to those who love Him. He is salvation.

He is patient. What are you thankful for today?

In Matthew 6, Jesus preaches his most famous sermon-The Sermon on the Mount. In this sermon we are taught what God desires for us to pray to Him: His will. It holds my life verse.

"But seek first His kingdom and His righteousness, and all these things will be given to you as well."

Matthew 6:33

Many years ago, I prayed a bold prayer. In my desperation to grow in wisdom and discernment, I asked the Lord to "humble me like Christ." Yes, those words slipped from my mouth, and as they reached my ears, I was terrified. I felt the fear of the Lord in a way I'd never experienced before. I even asked myself, "What does it look like to be humbled like Christ?" Considering what we know through biblical accounts, it starts with surrender.

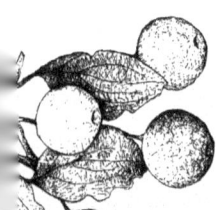

WEEK 1: DAY 4

The Bible tells us that we are made in the image of Christ. We are to be transformed, renewed by The Word and not only that, we are to die to our own desires **(Romans 8:13)**.

Read **Isaiah 53**

Consider what is means to be humbled like Christ and use the space below.

Reflecting on **Matthew 6:33** requires me to repent because I must admit that there was a season when I searched for the *all*, missing to seek Him first. With time I began to understand that to be more like Christ, to be humbled like Christ means a life of self-denial in all things.

In your search to "Count it All Joy!" What are you seeking first each day? Is there an all you are expecting? We are to seek and glorify God in all we do for His purposes.
The "all" includes the promises that follow.

WEEK 1: DAY 4

Promises Fulfilled

It's important not only to read the Word, but to write it out as a practice that helps etch it into our hearts. When my husband and I lived in Hawaii, about eight weeks before heading to our new duty station in Germany, I met a loving and kind woman named Sue. Sue runs a nonprofit ministry under Calvary Chapel Pearl Harbor. She ministered to my heart during a season of my life when I needed a compassionate listener. One day, during Bible study, she said, "Write it out."

I looked at her, puzzled. Then she said,

"The only way for you to get these words in your heart is by

writing them out and on your heart."

In our search to "Count it All Joy," we will uncover treasures of promises throughout the following verses. Write them out and underline the treasures you find. Remember to use your treasure box. Yes, as I write this study from Fort Huachuca, Arizona, I too am writing them out and am praying for you.

Treasures of God's Promises

Numbers 23:19

Joshua 23:10

WEEK 1: DAY 4

Psalm 119:41

Psalm 119:50

Psalm 119:57-58

2 Samuel 7:25-26

God's promises are an overflow of his grace and there is always room to learn and grow. There's so much more treasure to find. We've only uncovered the beginning of God's promises. Throughout the following week, we will continue to dig into His Word as we have written them on our hearts. Remember that having stood the test of faith we are blessed because 'he who promised is faithful.' Continue to 'Count It All Joy!'

You are Crowned in Beauty,
Kimberly

NOTES

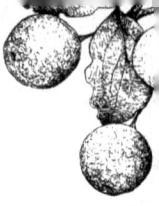

WEEK 1: DAY 5

Surrender and Availability

As you've journeyed through this week, one of my hopes is that you are beginning to notice aspects of your character—traits you might not have fully recognized before. Friend, you have been uniquely crafted by an all-knowing Almighty God, who sees *you*, knows, and has provided. If you're still questioning why we're here, let's prepare ourselves to receive the revelations God has for us in this pursuit of "Counting It All Joy."

"James, a servant of God and of the Lord Jesus Christ, wrote:
'Consider it pure joy when you face trials of many kinds because you know that the testing of your faith produces perseverance. Let perseverance finish its work so that you may be complete, not lacking anything. And if any of you lack wisdom, let him ask of God, who gives generously to all without finding fault."

(James 1:2-5)

At the core of who you are, God has placed desires—deep, God-given desires.
To bring them to fruition, we must be fully surrendered to Him.

Recently, I have accepted that when undergoing a trial, every day tasks become a struggle. Things like cooking a good meal or keeping to my routines. My mind floods with turbulent emotions that disrupt progress in other areas of my life. I know we are not promised a perfect life, but sometimes it'd be nice for smooth sailing.

WEEK 1: DAY 5

This is why it is important to be rooted and established in the faith. Having trusted friends who pray with you enrich your relationship with the Lord. To seek the Lord for guidance and wisdom and as it we have read in James 1, *"God will give it to you."*

One of the traits God has given me is compassion, and through it, I've learned the importance of being available. Because others have been available for me, God has also gifted me with compassion but it wasn't always this way. At times, my availability was a coping mechanism—a way to avoid addressing the things I needed to work on within myself. In retrospect that was a disservice to the Lord as filling my schedule only masked what I needed to be unmasked.

With time and reflection I surrendered and began my healing journey.

What is your story?

How do you use your time?

Are you available to others?

Who are you accountable to?

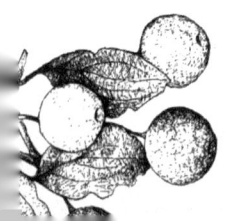

WEEK 1: DAY 5

What is your initial reaction when faced with a trial?

Do you make yourself available to God?

Outside of this study, how else do you fill your time?

Read the following verses.

Isaiah 6:8

Philippians 2:3

1 Corinthians 10:24

When Isaiah stood before the Lord and answered that he would go, he did so after confessing the state of his heart through his lips. Words matter. Thankfully God is a God of grace and mercy, who extended it to Isaiah. If we dig deeper this also speaks to the heart of man. Self-righteousness can keep us from hearing from the Lord. It can hinder relationships, later leading to pride. Isaiah confessed his sin.

Reread Philippians 2:3 and 1 Corinthians 10:24 and consider ways you can better serve the Lord for his purposes. God acts. He speaks. He is faithful. He fulfills. He does not change His mind

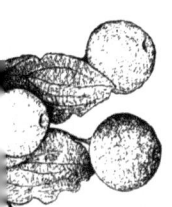

WEEK 1: DAY 5

He fights for us. His love is unfailing. He offers salvation. He brings comfort. These reminders of who God is and His promises will help us as we dive deeper in the weeks to come.

2 Peter 3:8-9

"But do not forget this one thing, dear friends: With the Lord a day is like a thousand years, and a thousand years are like a day."

This verse is incredibly comforting. Think about it for a moment. God is patient with us. There are times in life when we dread the alarm going off or want to rush through a season of refining, but this verse reminds us that when we remain available, it will serve a purpose. If one day is like a thousand years, how will you move forward in learning to "Count It All Joy"?

God has been speaking to you.

This week, we began with self-reflection, and it's crucial that we approach God's throne of grace with humility—searching our hearts. Remember, the One who formed us is the all-knowing God.

Looking out the window at the grandiosity of the Huachuca Mountains, I'm often reminded of

Isaiah 54:10:

"Though the mountains be shaken, and the hills be removed, yet my unfailing love for you will not be shaken, nor my covenant of peace be removed," says the Lord, who has compassion on you.

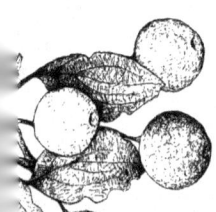

WEEK 1: DAY 5

I'm reminded that God Most High created the mountains.

Take time this week to admire the beauty that God has given us.

I am sure He has spoken a word of affirmation to you through someone else, reminding you that He is **El Roi—the God Who Sees.**

It's okay if you're still growing in your understanding of the sovereignty and regency of God. I was once hungry to understand, and I'm still on that journey.

One thing I continue to do is allow God to shape, mold, and grow me into godliness. The truth is, I am still learning to be content in every season of my life.

In the coming weeks, we'll explore how figures like Abraham, Elizabeth, Hannah, Mary, and Joseph, made themselves available to God's purposes through what I will call "joy filled surrender." The more I read their stories, the more I understand what it means to "Count It All Joy!"

You are deeply loved, and you are Crowned in Beauty,

Kimberly

NOTES

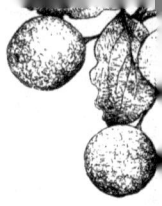

NOTES

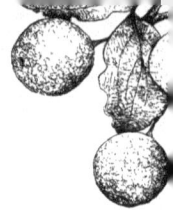

WEEK 2

The Father of Nations
Abraham

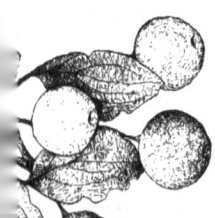

WEEK 2: DAY 1

Abraham, The Father of Nations

"Go! Go to the land I will show you."

— **Genesis 12**

In other words…Go! to everywhere I send you, do what I say, and by the way, you'll know when you get there, but I won't tell you exactly where (emphasis added).

Today, we are introduced to Abram who will later be known as Abraham the father of nations. We'll journey through lands, battles, and see promises unfold along the way.

Genesis 12, "The Lord had said to Abram, 'Go from your country, your people, and your father's household to the land I will show you.' So Abram went, as the Lord had told him, and Lot went with him. Abram was 75 years old when he set out from Haran."

We don't know much about his upbringing. Yet, he was called to leave the land his father, Terah had chosen to settle in. For reference, you can read **Genesis 11:26-32**.

WEEK 2: DAY 1

At 75 years old, Abram set out for a land that was unknown to him—the land of Canaan. When he arrived, the Lord appeared to him, and there Abram built an altar.

Has there been a moment in your life where a seed of hope was placed in your heart? Did you walk in obedience through that time or did you try to pave your own way? Did you live that season out with joy?

Abram's story teaches us about the beginning of a life of obedience and joy. He went without knowing the exact destination, but once he arrived, he built an altar as an act of worship.

The Significance of Altars

Altars play a significant role in the Bible. The first altar we read about in Scripture is in **Genesis 8:20**, after the flood. Noah built an altar to the Lord and sacrificed burnt offerings.

Let's read: Genesis 8:21–9:17.

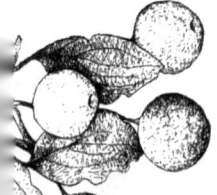

WEEK 2: DAY 1

The covenant God made with Noah still applies to us today. The Bible tells us that when Noah built the altar and offered sacrifices, it was a "pleasing aroma" to the Lord.

Earlier in the week one, I shared about my experience with the occult. In this false worship practice, Santeria, altars are built for the purposes of making offerings to a deity. Altars to deities, false gods, slowly steal away your joy and embed fear into you. These deities eventually bring oppression into your life. The main goal of these false gods are to capture your soul through fear, have you deny Christ and reject the gift of receiving eternal life.

The Significance of Altars

According to the biblical dictionary, an altar is a place, often made of stone, where sacrifices are offered. If you head over to **Genesis 3:20** you will read about the fall of man and the first sacrifice.

WEEK 2: DAY 1

What was placed on an altar? In ancient times, according to **Leviticus 17:11**,

'the life of a creature is in its blood,'

and it was through blood that atonement, forgiveness of sin was made.

But the ultimate act of worship at the altar was not just about

sacrifice—it was about reverence and honoring God.

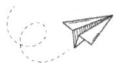

Reflecting on My Own Altars

When I gave my life to Christ, I learned that my life had to become a living sacrifice to God—just as **Romans 12:1** tells us:

"Therefore, I urge you, brothers and sisters, in view of God's mercy, to offer your bodies as a living sacrifice, holy and pleasing to God—this is your true and proper worship."

The Lord may not have told me specifically to go to an unknown land like He did with Abram, but He did tell me to "seek first the kingdom of God" **(Matthew 6:33)**. This call to surrender has been a lifelong journey—just as Abram's was.

As you think about the beginnings of your own life of surrender, can you identify a specific moment of overwhelming joy that you knew was worthy of worship to the Lord?

WEEK 2: DAY 1

Let's take a moment to build a written altar—a declaration of worship to God as we step into this unknown land with Abram. Dig deep into the treasures of God's promises.

Over the next few days, we will walk closely with Abram, who later becomes Abraham, and observe the altars he built, exploring the covenant promises of God, and a life of surrender and joy.

 **For Your Heart**

My friend, stay the course, and dive deep into God's Word each day. As **James 1:25** encourages us, let's remain teachable and continue to live a life that counts it all joy.

You are Crowned in Beauty,

Kimberly

NOTES

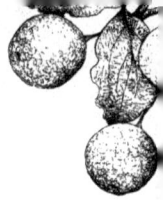

WEEK 2: DAY 2

From the Call to the Altar

Genesis 12 sets the stage for the unfolding of God's covenant promise of redemption. It introduces us to Abram, who will later become known as Abraham the father of nations. God calls Abram with these words:

"Go from your country, your people, and your father's household to the land I will show you."

We don't hear much else about Abram's early life. We only know that he was the son of Terah, and his family had settled in a place that wasn't part of God's original plan.
(For reference, read Genesis 11:26-32.)

At 75 years old, Abram steps out in faith to an unknown land. This land was Canaan. When he arrived, the Lord appeared to him and said, "To your offspring, I will give this land." And so, Abram built an altar to the Lord. Abram's story marks the beginning of a life of obedience and loyalty. He didn't hesitate. He simply went, and when he arrived, he built an altar as a sign of his worship and devotion to God.

 For Your Heart

Blessed Lord, Almighty God, the one who is, the God of promises, the Creator of

WEEK 2: DAY 2

heaven and earth, our Deliverer, who is righteous and mighty. The One who calls us into the deep. Today we are here to grow closer to you. Lead the way into helping us understand your Word more as we find joy in the right now. Amen

The Bible warns of ways joy is stolen from us, what some call "joy killers." These joy killers keep us from a life that is intended to honor the Lord.

Read Philippians 4:8.

What are you allowing in your life that is keeping you from following through on what God has shown you of your purposes for Him?

How is that specific thing robbing you of opportunities to go for God?

My Journey to the Altar

As I reflect on the altars I once built in my life, I understand that they were altars of fear that were built through monetary means and animal sacrifices all in the search for truth and peace. At the time, I genuinely believed I was doing the right thing. But in hindsight, I see that I was losing pieces of my peace and soul to a ruthless principality.

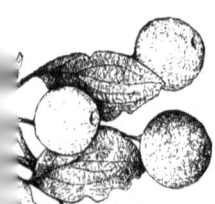

WEEK 2: DAY 2

Then, one day I surrendered my life to Christ. My life became a living sacrifice, dying to the things I once knew before Christ. I turned to Scripture, which began to purify my heart and mind. I understood that an altar is meant to be a place of honor and worship to God, through and because of Jesus Christ.

Let's reflect for a moment. As we have learned an altar is a place where sacrifice is made. It can also be a place of remembrance where one worships God. As you think about your life, are there any false altars you may have built, whether knowingly or unknowing? It may not be similar to me, it can be placing pictures in a place in your home that you go to, meditate, and find yourself running more often to than God?

Dig deeper and consider if this area of your life has become an idol. A person or even a past experience can become something of idolatry. Are you willing to surrender it to God today? If so, take a moment to repent and worship God for who He is.

WEEK 2: DAY 2

Abram's Faith and Obedience

Abram, now known as Abraham, remained faithful in his worship, honoring God even when circumstances were difficult. God changed Abram's name to Abraham, marking a new chapter in his covenant relationship. Over the next days, we will continue to explore the promises God made to Abraham, which will lead us to the ultimate fulfillment of God's redemptive plan.

As we journey with Abraham, let us build our own altars in our hearts where we remember them but more so as an act of worship while seeking His promises and His presence.

Treasure of Trials

Over the course of Abraham's journey, he faced many trials. As I reflected on Abraham's journey I began to understand how God takes our trials and uses them to refine us. Read through the following passages and write down the trials in your "treasure of trials" chest.
I have written the first two.

- **Genesis 12:10-12: Sarai is taken from Abram**

- **Genesis 13:5-11: Abram and Lot are separated**

- **Genesis 14:1-16**

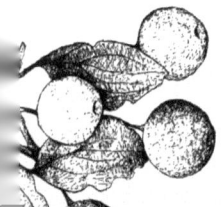

WEEK 2: DAY 2

- **Genesis 15:12-16**
- **Genesis 16:1-6**
- **Genesis 18:16-33**
- **Genesis 20:1-2**

These trials—though difficult—served to build Abraham's faith and strengthen his relationship with God and that is why they are a treasure. We see how God turned things around for His purpose and glory. Joy begins with reverence. Abraham remained faithful to the Lord because he loved Him and reverenced God.

 For Your Heart

Lord, we thank you for the examples of faith and obedience we see in Abraham's life. Help us to trust in your promises, to worship you with our whole hearts, and to build altars in our hearts of gratitude where we continually surrender to you. We pray for strength in our trials and the courage to follow through on the call you've placed on our lives. May we continue to seek your kingdom first, trusting that you will guide us every step of the way.

You are Crowned in Beauty,
Kimberly

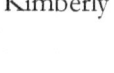

NOTES

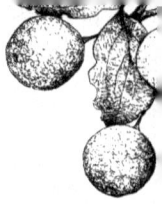

WEEK 2: DAY 3

The Cost of the In-Between

On Day 1, we began our journey with Abraham's call to an unknown land. Did you note the five blessings God promised to bring forth through Abraham's obedience? Along the way, we've met Pharaohs, read about new lands and famines, Sarai's abduction and return, kidnappings, altars of worship, and cities burning. The story of Abraham's life has been a source to me of deep reflection, especially in relation to understanding the role of a father.

Personally, reflecting on the bigger picture helps to see how God's strength guided Abraham through it all. It's a reminder that even in our own moments of uncertainty, our faith can grow as we look back and reflect on the Almighty God. He is the Creator of heaven and earth, the Deliverer, and the God who sees.

That brings us to today's focus:
Has there been an area of your life where you had a picture of what would be, but you're stuck in the "in-between" trying to make sense of it all? What instructions have you been given by God?

Wait on the Lord.

These were the instructions I received. As much as I wanted to fast-forward through certain chapters of my life, I have learned that it is often in the

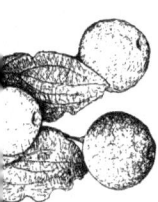

WEEK 2: DAY 3

"in-between" seasons where our character is sharpened. The more we focus on what God is revealing to us during these moments, the quicker we can learn to do everything with joy!

After Abram agrees to have a child with Hagar, Sarah's maidservant and Sarah's request, we see Hagar leave with her baby to the wilderness of Shur. It is there that the Lord reveals Himself to Hagar as *El Roi*, the God who Sees. If you need to revisit the story, check out **Genesis 16** or Day 3 of Week 1.

In **Genesis 16:11**, God's revelation to Hagar is striking. He reveals Himself as the God who sees, to an Egyptian woman—someone outside of the covenant. Yet, the promised blessing of an offspring will come through who God chooses, not Hagar's son.

This is an important moment for us to reflect on: When you see others being blessed with what you desire, how do you respond?

WEEK 2: DAY 3

This speaks to my heart because it's a reminder that God doesn't want anyone to perish. He desires for all to know Him, to be seen by Him, and to receive His blessings **(2 Peter 3:9)**. Even in difficult circumstances, the Lord's plans unfold in ways that we may not fully understand.

While Hagar and Ishmael are eventually told to leave, we read in **Genesis 21:8-20** that God still blesses Ishmael.

Now, let's move forward to **Genesis 17.** Here, God appears to Abraham when he is 99 years old and says,

"I am God Almighty; walk before me faithfully and be blameless. Then I will make my covenant between me and you, and will greatly increase your numbers"
(Genesis 17:1-2).

Just as He kept his covenant with Noah, he is now reaffirming his covenant with Abraham. As you read through these passages, look for the five blessings and promises God has made. Write them down in your Treasure Box.

- **Genesis 12:2-3,7**
- **Genesis 13:14-17**

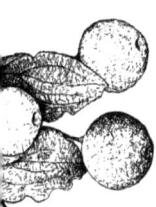

WEEK 2: DAY 3

†

Now, read **Genesis 15** and summarize the key points.

How many blessings and promises combined did you count in these recent verses?

I counted 18.

I began today's lesson by sharing a personal trial that I needed healing from. Growing up, I often felt unseen, unloved, and disconnected. But God in His mercy, placed people in my life who modeled for me the love of Abba Father—brothers and sisters in Christ who reminded me of the God of Abraham. With time, I began to hunger for a deeper understanding. I realized how I too, would fall under the same promises that God made to Abraham.

As we see in Abraham's journey, there's a cost to walking in these promises. For Abraham's descendants, that cost would be the circumcision of the flesh.

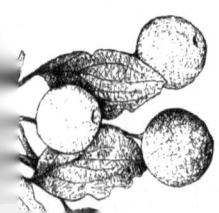

WEEK 2: DAY 3

We've dug deep into these foundational covenants, and it's worth remembering that the promises God made to Abraham still apply to us today. Tomorrow, we'll explore the concept of "a new name" in the covenant and witness the moment when Abraham, despite all odds, counted it all joy at another altar!

You are Crowned in Beauty,
Kimberly

NOTES

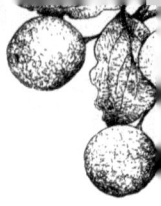

WEEK 2: DAY 4

A Covenant

We don't have much time today, so let's dive right in and uncover how God Almighty continued His covenant with Abram (Abraham).

Read Genesis 17.

Grab your pen and let's continue to gather treasures. What new blessings and promises can we add to the treasure chest?

I added: Father of many nations, a new name, kings will come from him, he will be fruitful. Nations will come from him. The covenant will extend to his descendants and future generations. The land of Canaan will be given to him and his descendants.

Everything in life involves an exchange—a condition. From there a result or consequence takes place.

Have you ever approached God with a "I will do this… if You do XYZ"?
Did you follow through on your commitment?

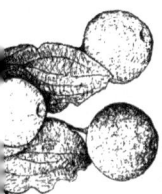

WEEK 2: DAY 4

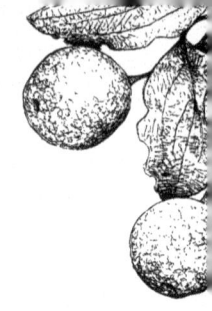

In **Genesis 17:9-22**, God gives Abraham specific instructions regarding the covenant, after changing his name. All men in Abraham's household, including slaves and those bought with money, were to undergo circumcision as a sign of the covenant.

Reading this, we understand that circumcision served as a physical marker to set God's people apart. Just as we are called to be set apart for God's glory, we too must "cut off the old man" (see verse 14).
The Lord then proceeds to give Sarai a new name—Sarah—and a promise that she, too, would bear a son. **(Genesis 17:15-16)**.

Joy!

Let's pause here for a moment. God had already promised Abraham 'joy' in **Genesis 15,** when He promised to be his "shield and his exceedingly great reward." The Lord continually pursued Abraham, showing him the greatness of what He would accomplish through him. The joy was God! The reward was God! That is Joy!

When Abraham hears that Sarah would bear a son in her old age, she laughs **(Genesis 17:17-18)**. Possibly, this laughter was an expression of disbelief but also an unexpected joy?

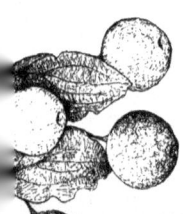

WEEK 2: DAY 4

Foreshadowing joy. We see that Abraham fell facedown, a sign of reverence, then he laughed. This joy would be embodied in Isaac, whose name literally means "laughter" **(Genesis 17:19)**. Imagine the scene: You've waited nearly 24 years for a promise, and then God asks you to make a physical sacrifice—cutting off your foreskin—and tells you that your son is still on his way. It's easy to understand Abraham's reaction, isn't it?

Let's go back to **verses 19-22** and add more to our treasure chest:

Sarah will bear a son and his name will be Isaac.
God will establish His covenant with Isaac and his descendants.
God will bless Ishmael, making him the father of 12 rulers and a great nation.

After God speaks to Abraham, He departs. Abraham follows through, circumcising himself and every male in his household as a sign of the covenant.

A Brief Summary of Genesis 18

The Lord appears to Abraham near the great trees of Mamre. As Abraham looks up,

WEEK 2: DAY 4

he sees three visitors. He rushes to meet them and offers them food, asking them to stay. As they wait, Sarah prepares a meal while eavesdropping, and one of the men says to Abraham, "I will surely return to you about this time next year, and Sarah will have a son" **(Genesis 18:10)**. Sarah, overhearing this, laughs to herself in disbelief. **Read verses 13-15**.

I believe it was a sign of an anticipated joy unbeknownst to Sarah. You know the kind that for some reason is believable, yet unsettling because it could happen? She had been waiting for a child, this promise she overheard about years prior.
Now, at the appointed time, God was bringing joy.

Perseverance is part of building our faith. Sarah's laughter wasn't just an expression of her disbelief; it was the seed of joy that would soon be realized. After the visitors leave, God reveals His plan to Abraham regarding the destruction of Sodom and Gomorrah. Abraham boldly intercedes on behalf of the cities, asking God to spare them for the sake of the righteous. He continues asking, "What if there are 50 righteous people? What about 45, 40, 30, 20, or even 10, righteous people?" **(Genesis 18:24-32)**. Abraham shows great boldness and compassion in pleading for mercy. Eventually, God destroys Sodom and Gomorrah, but Lot and his daughters are spared. However, Lot's wife, possibly consumed with the past, looks back and turns into a pillar of salt **(Genesis 19:26)**.

Looking back can hinder our progress. How often do we laugh in and unsettled joy that reveals something greater than what we see? If you've been holding onto things from the past that have delayed your joy, why not take a moment now to surrender them to the Lord?

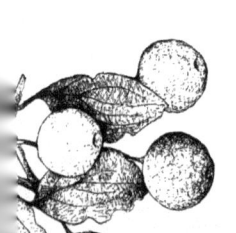

WEEK 2: DAY 4

If you haven't received Jesus as your Lord and Savior, remember that you have been removed from the physical circumcision. We are made alive in Christ by surrendering our old man, God knew Abraham's heart and gave him a new name, He has given you a new name too!

That is something worth celebrating!

In **Genesis 20**, King Abimelech takes Sarah as his wife after Abraham moves to Gerar. But God intervenes, telling King Abimelech to return Sarah to Abraham because he is a prophet. Abimelech agrees, and Abraham prays for the healing of Abimelech's household, and they are restored.

I've been hearing a prophetic voice say, "When others are being blessed around you, God is in your neighborhood; you're next!" This is such an encouraging reminder to worship. When God blesses those around us, it's a sign that He is near, and our blessing is on the way too!

WEEK 2: DAY 4

Read Genesis 21:1-6

Time passes, and the Lord is faithful to Sarah. Just as He promised he gave her a son, Isaac. Sarah declares,

"God has brought me laughter, and everyone who hears about it will laugh with me"
(Genesis 21:6).

Can you see how the very act of Sarah laughing, naming her son Isaac, and sharing her joy was a prophetic act of God's faithfulness? God weaves our stories into a masterpiece, filling our lives with joy just as He did for Sarah.

As you reflect on this promise fulfilled, take a moment to praise God for the joy He brings. Tomorrow, we will meet God at the final altar with Abraham and explore the depth of His covenant promises.

You are Crowned in Beauty,
Kimberly

NOTES

WEEK 2: DAY 4

The Promised Child

A new name, a blessed child—the child who brought laughter and joy: Isaac. When we trust in God's plan, even when things don't unfold as we imagined, the posture of our hearts reveals what we believe to be true about God. Despite the physical evidence or circumstances that challenge our understanding, the altar we build within ourselves must always remain one of faith, trust, and surrender. This is the journey of Abraham, and it is ours too.

After Isaac's birth, a pivotal moment in the life of Abraham occurs. Hagar and Ishmael are sent away, and we are reintroduced to Abimelech, the king, and Phicol, the commander of his army. They recognize God's hand in Abraham's life and approach him with a request to make a peace treaty, acknowledging God's favor over him. A dispute had arisen over a well Abraham had dug, and Abimelech's servants had seized it. To settle the matter, Abraham gives Abimelech seven lambs as a witness to the fact that he had dug the well. This covenant was made under the name of the Eternal God.

The Eternal God

Notice the theme emerging here. The Lord calls us to the unknown and that brings

WEEK 2: DAY 5

newness. He leads us to places, and when we walk faithfully through trials, calling on His name, we are blessed in the same way Abraham was. Abraham plants a tree in Beersheba and calls on God by a new name, "*El Olam*"—The Everlasting God, the one who is faithful and enduring.

Worship and Growth

As you have reflected on the life of Abraham, think about the trials that God has delivered you from. Write them down and take a moment to thank him for what you learned through them.

What are some of the trials that God has delivered you from?

Abraham's worship didn't end after the blessing; in fact, his worship grew deeper. As he calls on "El Olam," he reminds us that the worship of God must continue and deepen, especially after we receive our blessings. We grow through the trials, and with each victory, our faith is built upon itself. Test after test, God remains faithful, and we move closer to Him, just as Abraham did. Would you agree?

The Final Altar: The Test of Sacrifice

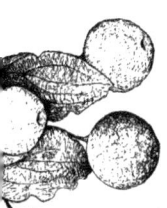

WEEK 2: DAY 5

As we conclude our week, let's focus on the final altar Abraham encounters—the altar of sacrifice. We find this in **Genesis 22:1-8**. In this passage, God gives Abraham a command that seems incomprehensible:

1. Take your son, your only son, whom you love, and go to the region of Moriah.
2. Sacrifice him there as a burnt offering on a mountain I will show you.

Abraham's response to Isaac's question about the lamb is a testament of unwavering faith. In **Genesis 22:8**, Abraham replies,

"God himself will provide the lamb for the burnt offering, my son."

This is faith! Even when God gives us the hardest commands, we can trust Him to provide.

Fatherhood and Faith

Throughout this week, I've shared parts of my personal journey with you. On Day 3, I spoke about my struggles with the role of fatherhood. For much of my life, I didn't have a stable, loving father figure. My father was absent for most of my childhood, and the times I did spend with him lacked depth and substance. My relationship with men,
was strained by years observing alcoholism,

WEEK 2: DAY 5

verbal abuse, and it instilled fear. The fear of abandonment, instability, the trauma's and carrying scars for decades made it a challenge.
But God's faithfulness, like Abraham's, became my reality. He sent men into my life who showed me what it meant to be fathered by God. Through those difficult years of rebellion and pain, God provided. Even though I didn't understand it then,
I can look back now and see His hand of provision.

The Test of Abraham's Faith

When Abraham reaches the place God had instructed him to go, he builds an altar and arranges the wood for the sacrifice. But as Abraham prepares to slay Isaac, God intervenes. **Genesis 22:12-15** recounts the moment where the angel of the Lord stops him, and we hear God's promise to Abraham. He declares:

"I swear by myself, declares the Lord, that because you did not withhold your son, your only son, I will surely bless you and make your descendants as numerous as the stars in the sky and as the sand on the seashore. Your descendants will take possession of the cities of their enemies, and through your offspring, all nations on earth will be blessed because you have obeyed me." **(Genesis 22:16)**

WEEK 2: DAY 5

In this powerful moment, God reaffirms His promises to Abraham—promises of blessings, of an inheritance that would touch every nation. Abraham's story is a model of obedience, a life of worship, trust, and reverence for God. He believed God would provide, even when it seemed impossible. When he lacked wisdom He asked God for it. He modeled **James 1:5** for us. We can all find ourselves in situations where obedience is hard, where faith is tested. But just like Abraham we can trust that God will provide.

What are you offering up to the Lord today?
What recent trials have you faced, and where might you be missing what God is doing right in front of you?

Imagine the relief and joy Abraham felt when he looked up and saw the ram caught in the thicket, a provision from God. He named the place "*The Lord will Provide,*" Jehovah Jireh **(Genesis 22:14)**. Abraham's life was one of surrender, a life full of worship and trust in the Lord's provision.

WEEK 2: DAY 5

His journey was challenging and is a testament to the faithfulness and provisions of God. In the midst of challenges—through battles, family struggles, and personal loss—God was present. Through it all, Abraham's heart was surrendered and his faithfulness was rewarded.

Reflecting on his journey is one of the many blessings God has given us while we find joy in surrendering all that we love, to God. Just as He provided for Abraham He will provide for us. Each trial, each sacrifice, each act of worship builds a foundation of faith that can be trusted.

I'm so blessed that we are learning to "Count it All Joy!" together.

You Are Crowned in Beauty,

Kimberly

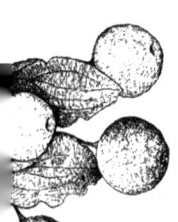

NOTES

NOTES

WEEK 3

Longing, Waiting & Surrender

Hannah

WEEK 3: DAY 1

Hannah: Longing, Waiting & Surrender

Where we come from truly matters. It shapes who we become. I may not be the only one who when driving through certain places, feels a wave of nostalgia, remembering things like, "I remember when…" I grew up in a small village near the border of another state. That village still lives on in my memories, even though it has drastically changed and most of the people I knew have either moved away or we've lost contact. Occasionally, I visit the few family and friends that still live there.

I remember sitting quietly in the chapel of Holy Rosary Church, while my mom visited with a friend. It was a peaceful. There was something about sitting in the chapel that brought me peace. It was there, in those quiet moments, that my love for prayer began to grow. This may have been when the Lord first called me to be an intercessor.

At home, I didn't see much prayer, just a few candles and pictures at the end of the hallway, honoring loved ones. Our Thanksgiving dinners were the only times we'd pray "thankful" prayers. I also remember visiting my cousins across the hall, where I could hear my cousin's grandmother crying out to God in prayer. I will never forget the raw sincerity in her cries, as she poured out her heart to the Lord.

Last week we camped out with Abraham and reflected on the altars of worship.

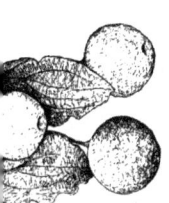

WEEK 3: DAY 1

Recall moments in your life that became memorial stones, marking your faith even in subtle ways.

As you reflect on these moments can you say that these moments helped you to count them as joy-filled moments?

Today, we begin a journey of faith with a woman whose love for the Lord was so deep, she was misunderstood at the altar of worship. She poured out her heart, not caring who saw or heard her, because all she wanted was for the Lord to hear and answer her prayers.

Her name was Hannah, which means "grace" or "favor." She was the wife of Elkanah, a Levite priest from the tribe of Ephraim. Why does it matter that she was married to an Ephraimite priest and also from the Levite priesthood?

Because, God's hand is extended to all, and He does not play favorites **(Romans 2:11)**. No one is exempt from trials in life—not even Elkanah and Hannah, two people that some would say had access to God's presence.

Let's jump right into our treasure hunt and open our hearts for God's guidance and revelation.

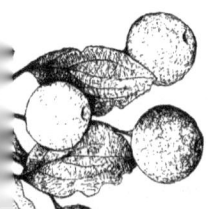

WEEK 3: DAY 1

 ## For Your Heart

Lord, my Counselor, the God of Abraham, Isaac, and Jacob—Almighty, Sovereign God—I thank you for your daily grace and mercy. I thank you for what you have already revealed to me and will reveal. Father, I ask for your wisdom to guide me, as you reveal more of yourself in this season. Help me live a life that counts it all joy. In Jesus' name, Amen.

Let's journey together through 1 Samuel 1:1-2. After reading these verses think about how Elkanah gave Hannah a double portion to encourage her and show her love. And, as you reflect where can you say you are asking Lord for wisdom and giving abundantly, trusting that God will bless the blessings you give to others. Write it in the space below.

On the contrary, Hannah had a desire for motherhood. The double portion she received from Elkanah kept her from joy in the Lord. When someone gives of themselves to encourage, whether through tangible items or acts of service, we may miss out on a blessing. When have you received a "double portion" and looking back see that there was a bleesing in disguise? Or maybe you did see the blessing and are thankful God encouraged you through it. Reflect on that time below.

WEEK 3: DAY 1

Continue reading 1 Samuel 1:3-7.

These verses speak deeply to my heart. I can relate to Hannah's experience. My husband and I tried for many years to conceive, but God didn't allow it. As I have read Hannah's story many times I have asked myself, "Why would God, in His sovereignty, not allow his servant to conceive? Why would Hannah have to endure such suffering and mockery, especially when she was made to sit with her rival Peninnah, Elkanah's second wife?"

While my rival wasn't a "second wife" like Peninnah, I had my own struggles. I had to endure years of hearing, "Our women are fertile," or comments about pregnancy from people I had just met. I was invited to baby showers and celebrated the joys of others, yet in those moments, I felt like an elephant in the room. Many people knew I longed for a child, and moments where it seemed there was an unspoken misconception that being childless meant I didn't want to be around children when people would actually say things like—"It might be too hard for you." The comments and assumptions were endless.

Does this story remind you of an opportunity that didn't come to fruition, or a door that you prayed to be opened, only to find it shut? Can you think of times when the enemy used people or situations to create insecurity, causing you to doubt God's goodness?

How did you react to those moments?

Hannah wept so bitterly that she could not eat.

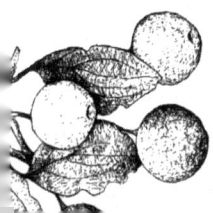

WEEK 3: DAY 1

We all reach a point of desperation, and may I remind you that sometimes that desperation leads to surrender—a surrender to the Sovereign God who sees and knows your heart's cry. Praise Him for today, and continue to find joy in every moment, trusting that his promises cover you with a love like no other.

 **<u>For Your Heart</u>**

My Sovereign King, you who hold my friend's heart in your hands, I pray for peace today. I pray that your oil of joy would overflow in the surrender of today. May they continue to seek you, and may you open their eyes to the treasures you have for them in this season. You are faithful, Lord. In Jesus' name, Amen. I'll meet you back here tomorrow.

You are Crowned in Beauty,
Kimberly

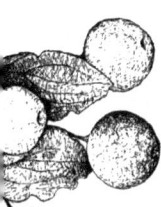

NOTES

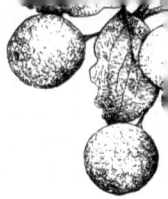

WEEK 3: DAY 2

Help My Unbelief

"Lord, help my unbelief. I see you in the details, but somehow, I find myself doubting you for this one thing. You can do it, but what about this? Do you see how much it hurts? Lord, help my unbelief."

The Bible tells us that year after year, Hannah went up to the house of the Lord with her husband, Elkanah, and Peninah. Year after year, Hannah carried the shame of her barrenness, holding her sorrow in silence. In **1 Samuel 1:6-8,** it says that she cried out to the Lord, but kept her heart's pain hidden, holding her tongue, and fasting in her grief.

The enemy is a taunter and the father of lies.

How do you react when provoked? Would you, like Hannah, get up and leave the table, or would you choose to fight from a place of surrender, trusting in victory?

As you read **1 Samuel 1:3-8,** what name of the Lord do you see?
Write them down and place them in your treasure box.

WEEK 3: DAY 2

Here, we encounter a name of God we've seen before, Yahweh Sabbath, Lord of Host. Let's reflect on its significance. LORD, Yahweh, the unpronounceable name of God. This name speaks to the deep, intimate relationship we are invited into with God. Years ago, I came across a social media post that suggested every time we breathe, we are speaking God's name. Whether or not that's true, we know from Genesis 1 that the Ruach—God's breath—hovered over the unformed earth and that same spirit later gave life to Adam.

There's much debate about the exact meaning of God's unpronounceable name. Some say it means "*I Am*" or "He who is." We also read in the book of Exodus **(see Exodus 3)** that God tells Moses, "*I Am who I Am.*" He is the Self-Existent, Eternal God who always has been, and always will be.

Hannah's story contributes a pivotal moment to the story of God. Though her husband loved her and gave her a double portion, it was the Lord who had closed her womb. And yet, even in her anguish, Hannah's faith stood firm. She prayed to God, knowing that He was El Shaddai, the All-Sufficient God, the God who sees, and the One who is faithful.

Read 1 Samuel 1:9-11 again.

Hannah's prayer reveals something profound. Her request is not one of demanding, but of surrender. In her prayer, she speaks to the God she knows: the Lord Almighty.

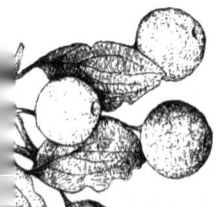

WEEK 3: DAY 2

Let's take a moment to treasure hunt and reflect on the words she uses:

"And she made a vow, saying, 'Lord Almighty, if You will only look on Your servant's misery, and remember me, and not forget Your servant, but give her a son, then I will give him to the Lord for all the days of his life, and no razor will ever be used on his head.'"

Vow, Lord Almighty, Look, Remember, Not forget, Give.
What do these words tell us about the posture of Hannah's heart?

Hannah's vow is bold, a prayer from the depths of her being. But more than a request, it's an offering. She understands that if the Lord grants her request, it is not for her own glory, but for His. The Lord remembers Hannah's heart, and He responds. This prayer of surrender doesn't just ask for a son but acknowledges the God who sees and is always faithful. **Psalm 34:6** reminds us that God knows our hearts even in our deepest moments of anguish.

What has been your prayer? How many times have you placed the same request at the altar, asking for the same thing, only to go unanswered? Take a moment to reflect on your own prayers. Are they prayers of surrender, or do you still

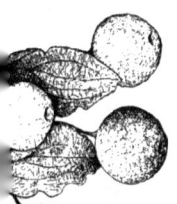

WEEK 3: DAY 2

hold onto control? Are you seeking God's will or your own? In your season of waiting or frustration, have you allowed God to change your desires to align with His?

During my own season of longing, I wrestled and cried bitterly many times. I was disillusioned with thinking I could control what was clearly outside of my grasp and struggled to surrender my will to God about being childless. But as I spent time in prayer, I learned that even in my frustration, God was working to transform my heart, much like He did with Hannah.

Now, Take an honest inventory of your heart. Are there areas of frustration or jealousy where you struggle with others' blessings? Have you ever felt like Hannah, questioning God's timing or will? Who are the "Peninahs" in your life—those who provoke or tempt you to doubt? Take a moment to bring these thoughts to the Lord.

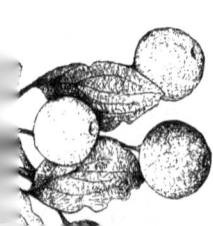

WEEK 3: DAY 2

 **Prayer of Repentance**

Lord, I confess the times I've allowed offense to harden my heart. Forgive me for doubting your timing and your goodness. I lay down my frustrations and the seeds of bitterness that may have grown in my heart. Help me trust you more deeply, knowing that you, the All-Sufficient God, see me and know the desires of my heart. Thank you for your faithfulness. In Jesus' name, Amen.

Friend, I want to encourage you, to 'Count It All Joy' as you walk in faith through your trials, knowing that God is working in you and through you. Remember, the Lord does not withhold anything from us. He gives without finding fault more so when our desires align with His purposes. El Shaddai, the All-Sufficient God, knows what we need and will provide in His perfect timing. Your journey is a testimony of His faithfulness, live it out for him. Trust in His plans, and surrender your heart fully to His will.

You are Crowned in Beauty,
Kimberly

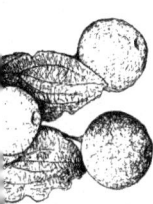

NOTES

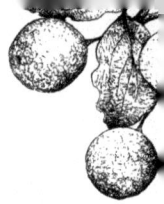

WEEK 3: DAY 3

<u>A Woman of Virtue, Loyalty, and Grace</u>

When we make a vow to the Lord, we must honor it, or we will face the consequences. Hannah's prayer was both genuine and prophetic.

Friend, I am so proud of you for being here, standing firm in faith. I pray that you approach God with the same boldness that Hannah displayed in her walk of obedience and reverence to the Lord. Even when it's hard, remember what **Psalm 28:7** says, *"The joy of the Lord is my strength."* He desires for us to delight in Him and be joyful in His presence.

In **1 Samuel 1:14**, Hannah is accused of being drunk. Hannah prayed and Eli, the priest, was sitting at the doorpost of the Lord's house, watching her lips move but hearing no words.

"How long are you going to stay drunk? Put away your wine." "Not so, my lord," Hannah replied. "I am a woman who is deeply troubled. I have not been drinking wine or beer; I was pouring out my soul to the Lord. Do not take your servant for a wicked woman; I have been praying here out of my great anguish and grief."

WEEK 3: DAY 3

1 Samuel 2, we read that Eli rebuked his own sons for failing to honor the Lord's house, and his passive leadership led to the removal of the priesthood from his family. Considering what we know of the sons of Eli the priest, it seems that many people frequented the Temple intoxicated which may indicate the type of response towards Hannah.

1 Samuel 1:15–16, We read that Hannah responded with grace and humility.

We all face moments when we are overlooked, judged or misunderstood. The Kimberly before Christ was a reckless, spontaneous, and adventurous person. But the day I laid my life down at the altar, I left that old version behind and began working on developing godly character while still embracing parts of my unique personality.

Have you ever poured out your heart to God like Hannah? Maybe you've been misunderstood or judged, even though you knew you were standing right with God in that moment.

Let's continue with verse 17: *Eli answered her, "Go in peace, and may the God of Israel grant you what you have asked of Him." And she said, "May your servant find favor in your eyes." Then she went her way, ate something, and her face was no longer downcast.*

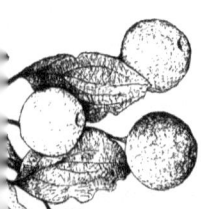

WEEK 3: DAY 3

Reflecting on Hannah's story begs the question, Was her longing only for a son, or was it more about entering into a deeper relationship with God? When we are going through trials our dependency of God should grow. It strengthens our faith. In essence what we are seeking is a desire that God has given us. Through it our relationship with Him grows. Years of watching others experience what she longed for herself, yet trusting in God's purpose, required faith. As we walk through life, we must trust that God will bring others along to strengthen our faith and agree with us in prayer.

Eli must have experienced a heart check when he heard Hannah say, "I am pouring out my soul to the Lord." Hannah didn't say, "I am distressed because I am barren," nor did she complain about Peninah mocking her. She didn't focus on her struggles; she focused on the Lord. Words have power. **Proverbs 18:21** says, *"The tongue has the power of life and death, and those who love it will eat its fruit."*

When we approach God's throne, His grace is extended to us, and with it, He gives us more grace. But this will cost us something—humility and the denial of self.

There were times in my life when I reacted in ways contrary to how Hannah responded. Offenses in my heart delayed my spiritual growth. Surrendering our thoughts and feelings, especially when feeling condemned, is hard. But we must surround ourselves with people who know the Word of God, stand firm in their faith and disciple us.

WEEK 3: DAY 3

Trials have a way of revealing areas of our hearts that need tending to. Thankfully, God refines us through the fire of those trails, and if we seek Him. When we do, He will give us wisdom and guidance.

When I finally surrendered my unbelief, I approached God in humility, praying a simple prayer: *"Lord, I trust You. I surrender this unbelief. If it's Your will that we walk this IVF journey, I will trust You. Regardless of the outcome, bring me your peace."*

Eli believed in Hannah's prayer, and he believed with her. My husband, family, and close friends stood by us in faith, praying for and with us.

Think about the people who have influenced you. Are you allowing them to speak into your life, to help you grow in faith? Who among them is standing with you in faith, fighting battles alongside you? Write their names below, and thank the Lord for them.

A Sacrificial Request

Hannah must have felt the faith in Eli's blessing, because when she left the house

WEEK 3: DAY 3

of the Lord, her face was no longer downcast, and she ate. She had been remembered by God. In time, her faith and her prayers were answered. A prayer filled with anguish can transform into a prayer of joy. As we read about Hannah, we see a woman who was full of reverence, wisdom, and faith. When she made her vow to the Lord, she kept it.

When we make a vow to the Lord, we must keep it.

My heart leaps with joy for Hannah, but I also weep, knowing that she had to follow through on the second part of her prayer. She was willing to sacrifice what she loved the most in order to honor her vow.

Joy is found in surrender.

The day I gave my life to Christ, I prayed, "Lord, I will do whatever you ask of me—just take me as far away as possible." That day there was an exchange.
What has been your sacrificial request?
What are you asking for and willing to give over to God?

WEEK 3: DAY 3

Go back to Week 2, Day 4, and read your reflection questions.

Has anything changed since then?

Has God given you a new outlook on what you wrote?

What do you remember most about it?

We need people like Eli to help build our faith. As we close today, I want to remind you that you are exactly where God needs you to be. It may not always feel that way, but your most trusted friends and confidants see it. If you don't have relationships like this, I encourage you to step out in faith and pray about who your trusted friend or mentor could be. You need a community to remind you, just as Eli reminded Hannah, that you can go eat because your days of weeping bitterly are over!

You are Crowned in Beauty,

Kimberly

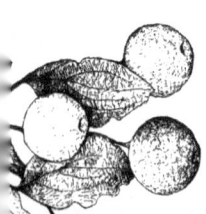

NOTES

WEEK 3: DAY 4

Remember Me, O Lord

"Lord Almighty, if only... Then I will give him to the Lord."

Hannah's prayer was a beautiful, selfless cry—a prayer of sacrificial surrender.

"Remember me, O my God, and do not forget, but give, and then I will give."

This was her vow, and it reflects the very essence of what it means to surrender to the Lord. To give back what was freely given. As we read about Hannah, we see a woman whose heart had truly encountered and reverenced the Lord. She received the blessing through Eli, and though her circumstances seemed unchanged, she knew her prayer had been heard. She went from sadness to joy, and in time, she gave birth to a son. She named him Samuel—a name that means, "Because I asked the Lord for him."

Read 1 Samuel 1:21-22

When you are in a place of complete surrender, there's always an expectation. Hannah's love for the Lord was so deep that we must pause and consider how she must have felt leading up to the moment when she would have to give Samuel back to God. Can you imagine being in her shoes, knowing that the child you prayed for and

WEEK 3: DAY 4

labored for would be dedicated to the Lord for life? There were no take-backs, no hesitation. Hannah was fully surrendered. **Deuteronomy 23:23** reminds us, "You shall be careful to do what has passed your lips, for you have vowed a vow to the Lord your God."

I think about my own prayers of surrender and how, over time, I've come to understand God as sovereign. If He willed something, I would honor my vow, just as I did back in 2008 when I gave my life completely to Him. What's interesting is that many times we say, "When God asks you…" God doesn't asks, He commands.

When we make a vow to Him, we must keep it. If He doesn't will it, then we must choose to continue honoring Him and growing in our dependence and love because of who He is. I remember a moment when my husband and I were having dinner, and I looked at him and said, "I'm ready to try. I'm going to call tomorrow and schedule the appointment to start this process."

Ten months earlier, when I visited the IVF clinic, they told me I had a 5% chance of a successful treatment. But when the time came, I rebuked that 5% and declared, "But my God will provide." Those six weeks starting on January 13, 2020, were some of the most intense, emotionally, yet peaceful times of my life. When I received the medication and began the treatment, I was at peace.

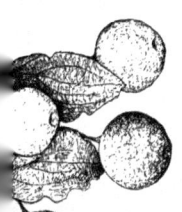

WEEK 3: DAY 4

The same God who heard Hannah's prayer is the same God who hears us today. The God of Abraham, Isaac, and Jacob is still Sovereign, and through Jesus Christ, His Spirit dwells in us. The perfect love that cast out fear is available to us through Christ, and it's that love that compelled Hannah to fulfill her vow.

Think about the promises you've made to God. Have you kept them? Is there any part of you that is hesitant to fulfill your vow? What might be keeping you from doing so? Finally, because I have asked myself this question I ask you to look within. Ask yourself if you trust God enough to make a promise and keep it?

Read 1 Samuel 1:20

When I think of Hannah holding her baby and preparing to dedicate him to the Lord, I picture her carrying him everywhere. Watching his first steps, and knowing that those little feet would soon walk on anointed ground. I often find myself reflecting on how much I need to grow in my faith, to rely fully on God, and to continuously surrender more to Him.

Read 1 Samuel 1:23-25

As Elkanah and Hannah prepared to make their sacrifices, they knew that soon their miracle would be dedicated to the Lord.

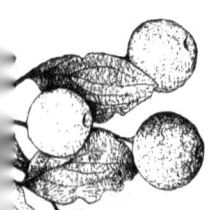

WEEK 3: DAY 4

My heart breaks for Hannah as I wonder if she ever thought,
"What if this is the only child God gives me, and now I must give him back to God?"

This question reveals the fragility of our mind, why we need to depend on God and why we must keep the Word close. When we begin to wander in our minds, we bring up imaginations. It also reminds me of how I struggle with control. I need Jesus more than ever, every single day.

Read 1 Samuel 1:26

Hannah became a living testimony of God's grace. She shared her story with Eli the priest, and in doing so, she magnified God's faithfulness and sovereignty. Our stories matter because they sharpen our faith and can draw others closer to God.

As we close, pause and bear witness to someone about what God has already done in your life. Share your story, or even write it down. There is always room for joy, even as you learn to 'Count It All Joy!'

You are Crowned in Beauty,
Kimberly

NOTES

WEEK 3: DAY 5

A Collection of Praise

Friend, as we approach the end of our time with Hannah, I want to pause for a moment and tell you how proud I am of you. God is even prouder of you! He knows you intimately—He created you, He formed you, and He gave you your unique character and personality traits. You are so special to Him, and He loved you before you were even born.

When Hannah stood in the house of the Lord, she did so with a heart full of praise, worship, and reverence. Her prayer is a beautiful declaration, filled with the names of God. Through her words, we see how deeply Hannah knew God. Even after dedicating Samuel to the Lord, the Spirit of the Lord filled her with joy and prophetic insight as she spoke blessings over her child in **1 Samuel 2:1-10.**

Go on a quick treasure hunt through **1 Samuel 2:8-10**, and fill up your chest. Below are the first two I found.

- Raises the poor
- He lifts the needy

WEEK 3: DAY 5

The Spirit of God gives us life and draws us nearer to Him. It sees the heart of man. God chose Hannah, a woman of unwavering faith, who stayed close to Him and honored Him with a promise. She gave her son Samuel to the Lord, and in doing so she set him on a path to serve God. Because Hannah put God first, Elkanah agreed that their son was God's gift, and they both believed in God's word **(1 Samuel 1:23)**.

1 Samuel 1:18-21

Hannah had no reservations about her vow to the Lord. Her heart must have overflowed with joy as she prepared to see her firstborn child. Every year, Hannah experienced the joy of knowing that the Lord had answered her prayer. Not only did God give her the son she so desperately desired, but He also extended His grace to her each year as she continued to fulfill her promise.

1 Samuel 1:27-28

The God who hears and sees is Sovereign.
He is our Provider, Protector, Almighty, and Most High.

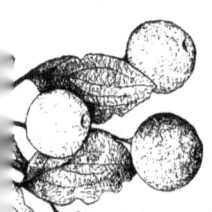

WEEK 3: DAY 5

The night before embryo transfer, as I drifted off to sleep,
I heard the words the Lord spoke to the prophet Jeremiah fall in my spirit:

"Before I formed you in the womb, I knew you; before you were born, I set you apart." Then I heard the Spirit of the Lord say, *"Your eyes saw My unformed body, and just as I saw yours, I see theirs, and you will too."*

(Jeremiah 1:5, emphasis mine)

I didn't fully understand at the time, but then God gave me a vision of an embryo under a microscope. The next day, my husband and I decided to transfer one healthy embryo, we had 2 by day 5. As the Embryologist prepared the syringe filled with the embryo, I finally understood what God had meant. That tiny tube contained a life, full of dreams and Gods purposes. When the embryo was implanted, the Embryologist pointed out a small bright light on the ultrasound screen. I had peace with and within me. Weeks later, that little bright light—embryo AA—successfully implanted and began to grow.

I will never forget standing over the kitchen sink, eight weeks post-treatment, with tears in my eyes. I lifted my gaze to God and whispered, "Lord, thank You for doing what man said couldn't be done. You took that 5% and provided. You gave me peace, and no matter the outcome, Lord, You did it, and he belongs to you." Though I didn't yet know the baby's gender, I could feel it in my spirit that we would have a boy. I knew that embryo AA was a gift from God—borrowed for a time, but ultimately belonging to Him.

WEEK 3: DAY 5

Your story, friend, is unique to you, just as mine is. Hannah's story is hers and yet meant to encourage us in The Lord. The beautiful thing about our individuality is that God uses each of us in different ways to encourage others and reveal His greater purpose.

Through our trials, He is glorified.

Hannah's story is a powerful reminder that the Lord is a God who requires honor, reverence, and a submissive heart—one that pursues Him for who He is. Just as Hannah was blessed in her surrender, we too can be sanctified through our trials, knowing that they lead us to joy and a deeper understanding of God's will for our lives. As you walk through life, I pray that you experience the same grace Hannah did. Let His joy and peace fill your heart, and may you always glorify His name in all that you do. Let Hannah's story encourage you to 'Count It All Joy,' knowing that through every trial, God is working out His greater purpose in your life.

You are Crowned in Beauty,

Kimberly

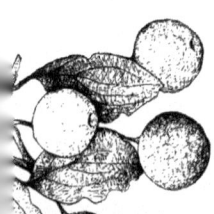

NOTES

NOTES

WEEK 4

The Righteous Servants

Elizabeth & Zechariah

WEEK 4: DAY 1

Elizabeth & Zechariah: The Righteous Servants

The stories of Abraham and Hannah represent surrender and joy in ways that, before embarking on this journey with them, I had not fully appreciated. I now see how deeply they counted all their trials joy! My understanding of God and my dependence on Him with time has increased, as it must for all. I see how profoundly their lives were part of God's story—and how our lives fit into His greater narrative. Their stories have shown what honor, faith, and perseverance look like in the life of an all-sufficient God.

Throughout my life, I've met many amazing, devoted, Christ-loving people. Some have struggled, their pasts keeping them in a place of complacency and brokenness. I've seen firsthand how holding on to the past can hinder growth. I've also met people who remind me of Terah, Abraham's father, who settled where it was comfortable. Yet, I believe there is always room for improvement.

When you consider the stories of the people around you, and see their righteousness, does it encourage you to move past your own past and pursue righteousness?

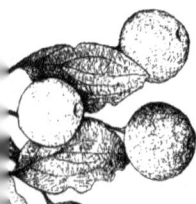

WEEK 4: DAY 1

I've also met people who grew up in church, with parents and grandparents who were faithful believers. They may not have a "radical" testimony as many see it, but their submission and faith are a testimony in themselves. It builds my faith when I see individuals who, though raised in the faith, faced hardships and realize that the faith they stood on was more about their family's belief than their own because it shows that no one has arrived.

No matter where you are in your faith journey, whether you have a radical testimony or not, the testimony of Jesus in your life is powerful in itself! There are those who are completely devoted to serving the Lord, living righteously in His sight and still face trials. These people were those who obeyed His decrees and commands, prioritizing the Lord in everything. They came from a priestly lineage, and God chose them for His glory. Zechariah and Elizabeth, are another perfect example of a life that, 'counted it all joy!"

Have you noticed a theme of time in God's plans as we read through the Bible? In life, we often feel like we should be following a timeline: at 25, graduated with a degree; at 30, married with kids, a house, and a steady job. Maybe a couple of horses, too.

I used to envision this, and I'll be honest—30 years old, three kids, a full-time job, and a house to care for? That doesn't sound like fun. Who's feeding the horse, making breakfast, cutting the grass, and managing a 40-hour workweek—all while trying to find time for the Lord?

WEEK 4: DAY 1

But God's timing—and the way He calls people—are a mystery in themselves. He is the God of Abraham, Isaac, and Jacob. The same God who chose the descendants of Aaron, from the priestly division, to usher in the one who would prepare the way for our Messiah, Jesus.

His timing spans thousands of years. To us, it seems long, but as **2 Peter 3:8** tells us, "a day is like a thousand years to the Lord." So, maybe it's only been two days in His sight. Yes, I'm being humorous, but my point is that God's timing is always best.

Before we embark on our treasure hunt this week, let's do a quick exercise. Take a moment to reflect on your life-changing moments—whether good or bad, recent or from years ago—and write them in the graph below from the beginning of your life.
This will help us see the bigger picture together. Focus on monumental moments of Faith where God intervened or walked you through those times.

Us the left side to gauge the Faith to Little Faith you had during the times you write down.

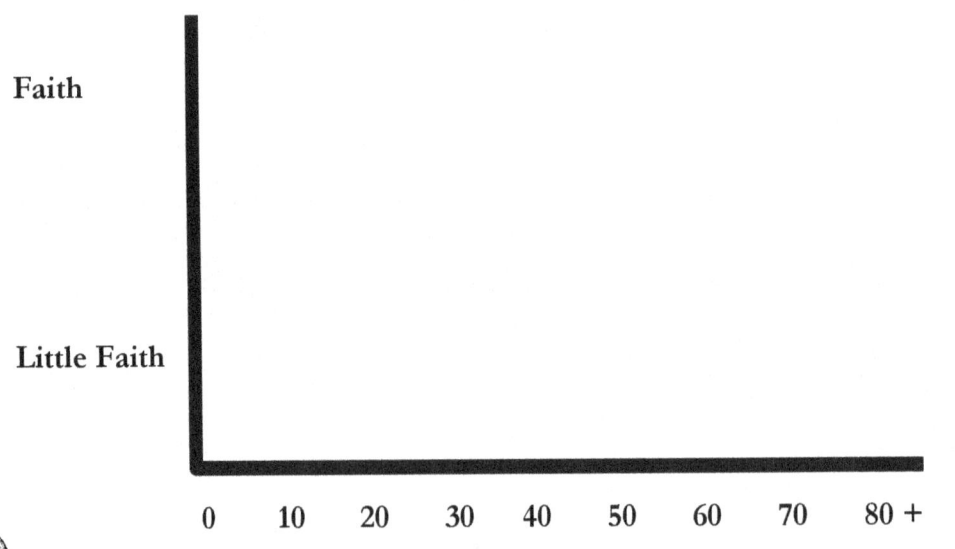

Faith

Little Faith

0   10   20   30   40   50   60   70   80 +

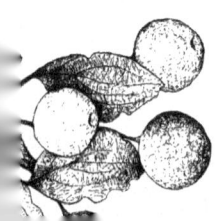

WEEK 4: DAY 1

Friend, He is not done with you yet. There is more to come. I truly believe that by now, your heart, like mine, has grown in joy toward the Lord as you look back at the living Word and see His hand in everything. This graph represents a life still in progress. God is not done with you. No matter the valleys you've walked through, He has never left you, and you are here. I'm so proud of you! Are you proud of who you are becoming on this journey? Write it down, because God knows your heart, and He sees your intentions as you learn more about Him.

Write this out today as a reminder- I am proud of myself!

_____

Because God's desire is for me to delight in Him, I pray, "Lord, continue to guide me to count it all joy!" In Jesus' name.

The **Book of Luke** begins with an encouragement to a fellow Christian named Theophilus. It was written to provide understanding of the life, ministry, and resurrection of Jesus, as well as His instructions for the people of the time. These teachings help us understand the gospel and how it fits into the grand story of God's redemptive plan for the world.

WEEK 4: DAY 1

Let's begin by reading Luke 1:1-7.

Some key takeaways from these verses are:

- Zechariah, the priest, and Elizabeth were both descendants of Aaron.
- They were righteous in the sight of God, observing all His commands and living blamelessly before Him.
- They were childless because Elizabeth could not conceive, and they were both advanced in age.

They were righteous before the Lord.

When you think about the word "righteousness," Define it and what does that look like to you? How important is righteousness in God's eyes, and what are His expectations for us?

There are times in life when God's response may be "not now." As you've been journeying with me these past few weeks and I've shared encouragement through my own trials, I still have a long way to go. Friend, we must be honest with ourselves—to examine our actions, words, and thoughts. And we must continuously remember that in Jesus, we have become a new creation. The past is gone, and the new has come (2 Corinthians 5:17).

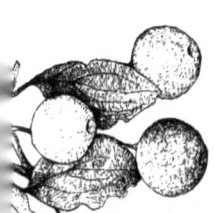

WEEK 4: DAY 1

To be counted as righteous begins with faith. Before we delve into the story of Zechariah and Elizabeth, let's revisit the Father of Nations: Abraham.

Finish today's lesson by jumping ahead to Hebrews 4 and reading the chapter. Then answer the questions below.

What is faith?

What is righteousness in God's eyes, and how am I honoring the Lord?

I pray that, in all you do today, you will seek the joy of being counted as righteous in God's sight, which is worth 'Counting It All Joy!'

You are Crowned in Beauty,

Kimberly

NOTES

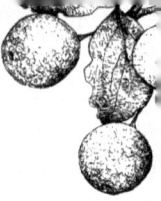

WEEK 4: DAY 2

Serving with Joy and Purpose

It is truly a privilege to serve the Lord and be a part of His house, to bless others through it and have the written Word in hand in order we do all things with joy! At least, that is how I picture those who came before us, and even those who serve with joy in their hearts today. When we reflect on yesterday's verse from **Luke 1:6**, we understand that righteousness begins in the heart, and God sees all.

Zechariah's Division: Abijah. Zechariah was on duty, serving as a priest before God.

Read Luke 1:11-17

If you're unfamiliar with the concept of being "chosen by lot," it refers to a divine decision made by drawing stones or objects, indicating God's will through the process. The person who draws the chosen object is the one selected for the task. As the people assembled to pray outside the temple, an angel of the Lord appeared to Zechariah.

"Do not be afraid," he said.

WEEK 4: DAY 2

When was the last time you heard something that spoke to the very core of your being and caught your attention?

These four words, "Do not be afraid," were first introduced in **Genesis 15**, before the covenant with Abraham was made. Now, we read them again as a messenger of God stands directly in front of Zechariah, bringing forth a divine declaration. God's plans call us to serve a greater purpose. Let's take a closer look at the following passages.

Read Luke 1:13-17

Quite the calling, don't you think? This is a perfect place to begin this week's treasure hunt. In the spaces above, place the words that describe who this son is and what he will do in your treasure chest. As a new creation in Christ, you are also called to "prepare the way of the Lord Jesus" to the world. This call, which was placed on John before his birth, also applies to you.

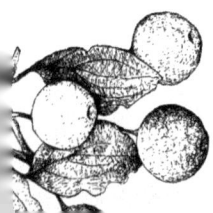

WEEK 4: DAY 2

Now, not in the same way as the spirit of Elijah, but in the spirit of Jesus Christ—the spirit of God, which John preached about.

Take a moment and go back to Week 1, Day 1. Do you remember the character traits you wrote down about yourself? Take a moment to reflect on the fact that before you were born, there was already a specific assignment on your life.

Do you know what that is? If so, how are you living it out? If not, take some time to explore and fill in the treasure chest.

Tomorrow, we'll do some deep digging as we explore who this angel is and why Zechariah's mouth was shut. Rejoice, friend! Rejoice because each day that God calls you to reflect and grow brings you closer to understanding how far you've come with Him. He is truly teaching you how to 'Count It All Joy!'

You are Crowned in Beauty,
Kimberly

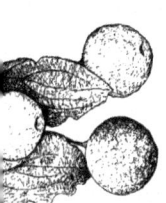

NOTES

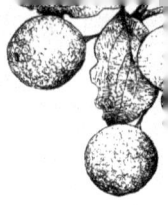

WEEK 4: DAY 3

Protected by Silence

Have you ever experienced something so overwhelming that it left you speechless? We've all likely had moments where words failed us, but I can't imagine it being to the extent of Zechariah's experience. When he entered the temple and fulfilled his priestly duties, the angel of the Lord appeared before him.

Read Luke 1:12

We can only wonder if Zechariah's petition to the Lord was for him and Elizabeth to conceive. I imagine their conversations went something like this:

Elizabeth might have said, *"Okay, Zechariah, the time for casting lots is here. Please pray that you're chosen so you can ask the Lord to bless us with a child,"* Zechariah might have reassured her, by saying, *"I promise you, Elizabeth, the Lord will give us a child. We love the Lord and honor Him. We've stood firm in faith, haven't we? He will make a way somehow, I know it."*

Now, I'm speaking for Elizabeth here, but I suspect Zechariah was just as desperate for a child. If he was ministering in the temple, he surely prayed for himself and his

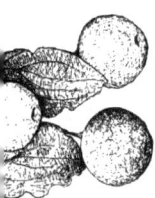

WEEK 4: DAY 3

wife as well. But when the angel of the Lord appeared, delivering the news that their prayer had been answered, Zechariah, caught up in disbelief, questioned how it could be since he and his wife were both old **(Luke 1:18–20)**. One could entertain, and I mean that lightly, that it was also his desire, and he "may" have said this as time was running out?

A Moment of Silence

Though righteous in the sight of God, Zechariah questioned the messenger of God. Yet, God, in His faithfulness, honored Zechariah's heart but chose to silence him for a time. The Lord shut his mouth to protect the integrity of the message.

Imagine, if Zechariah had been allowed to speak—do you think people would have laughed or ridiculed him? In his excitement, would others have doubted the divine message he received? God knows exactly why He does what He does, even when it doesn't make sense to us. Silence can be a profound gift when it serves a greater purpose.

There are times in our lives when God plants a seed or desire in our hearts, and in our excitement, we're eager to share it with others.

Have you ever shared a revelation prematurely?
Did it cause a delay or did the answer come immediately?

WEEK 4: DAY 3

I've certainly learned this lesson the hard way. In my excitement to see things come to pass, I realized not everyone will cheer you on in the same way. It's an unfortunate reality, but it happens.

When I was preparing for IVF. For the first few weeks, I kept it quiet—only a few people knew. But one week before my procedure, I shared with my Bible study group that I was undergoing treatment and needed prayers for God's will, no matter the outcome. Deep in my heart, I felt I would have a son—whether adopted or biological.

About 15 weeks later, I was 10 weeks pregnant, and when I ran into someone I had shared my journey with, their reaction was not as joyful as I had expected. It stung, and I was reminded to pray for them, not knowing what trials they might have been facing themselves. It also reminded me that there is a time and place to share, and not everything needs to be broadcasted.

Elizabeth's Hidden Joy

In **Luke 1:23-24**, we read that Elizabeth, like Zechariah, was fervently praying for a child. She had probably been trying to put on her best face for the community, even though her personal pain might have been palpable. Once she

WEEK 4: DAY 3

conceived, she remained hidden with God, praising Him for His favor. She declared, "The Lord has done this for me; He has shown His favor and taken away my disgrace among the people."

Her joy was rooted in the quiet strength that came from her relationship with the Lord.

Hidden with God is the perfect place to be, especially when we are walking through trials or navigating victory.

For a long time, my zeal for the Lord and His miracles in my life were misunderstood by others. At times, I felt like I had to prove my faith, for example by sharing addresses of bible verses I knew without second guessing. But I eventually realized that even those who have walked with the Lord for years often carry deep wounds that bring shame and guilt.

Even those who know Christ need Him daily.

Many of those who came before me, doing the hard work of faith, have given me the hope and courage to press on. They prepared the way for me to experience the freedom in Christ that I now understand. One day, I'll share more about that.

<u>Chosen for His Purpose</u>

It was God who chose Zechariah and Elizabeth for this moment in history, and it was

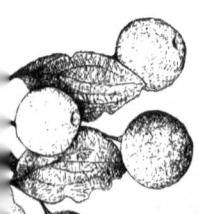

WEEK 4: DAY 3

all in His perfect timing. Years later their obedience would bring John—the forerunner to our Messiah. John was God's chosen vessel, tasked with preparing the way for Jesus. And through this miracle, God would bring great joy.

I am so thankful for the living Word of God. It's not just words on a page but a powerful, eternal truth. It brings hope, and my prayer is that you continue to run to it, counting it all joy, as you discover more of God's heart for you.

I encourage you to reflect on the beautiful ways God has chosen and called you. Like Zechariah and Elizabeth, you too have a purpose that aligns with His perfect timing. Though the journey may sometimes involve waiting or unexpected silence, trust that He is always at work, and He will bring His promises to pass in His time. As you journey through this week, may you find peace in the truth that God has chosen you for a purpose, and in Him, your joy is secure.

You are Crowned in Beauty,
Kimberly

NOTES

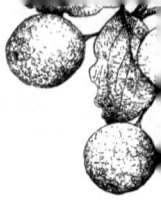

WEEK 4: DAY 4

The Lord's Favor

Favor is not earned; it is given freely. There is nothing we can do or say that will change the way God extends His favor to us. Whether it's through a new opportunity, career advancement, or a simple act of kindness.

What is the favor of God on your life? Be specific.

Read Luke 1:26-38

How is God's favor displayed in the story of Mary and the foretelling of the birth of Jesus?

"For no word from God will ever fail."
God is faithful, and the favor He brings comes in His perfect timing.

Read Luke 1:39-45

In these verses, Elizabeth tells Mary that she is blessed because she believed that the Lord would fulfill His promise to her. But why does she also say that Mary is "highly favored"?

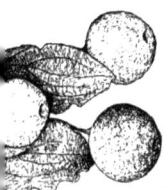

WEEK 4: DAY 4

Consider how, upon hearing Mary's voice, Elizabeth's baby leaped in her womb. Elizabeth believed, and she agreed with the Holy Spirit. Just as it was said in **Luke 1:15,** the work of the Holy Spirit was taking place before her very eyes, and she was blessed to witness it and to help Mary in carrying out God's plan.

Mary's Song

46 And Mary said, "My soul magnifies the Lord, 47 and my spirit rejoices in God my Savior, 48 for he has looked on the humble estate of his servant. For behold, from now on all generations will call me blessed; 49 for he who is mighty has done great things for me, and holy is his name. 50 And his mercy is for those who fear him from generation to generation. 51 He has shown strength with his arm; he has scattered the proud in the thoughts of their hearts; 52 he has brought down the mighty from their throne and exalted those of humble estate; 53 he has filled the hungry with good things, and the rich he has sent away empty. 54 He has helped his servant Israel, in remembrance of his mercy, 55 as he spoke to our fathers, to Abraham and to his offspring forever."

What treasures can we uncover in these verses? I wrote the first one I found.
- "God is her Savior, the Mighty One; Holy is His name."

WEEK 4: DAY 4

Mary's song is one of praise and adoration, but it is also one of surrender and a recognition of her need for a Savior.

Read Luke 1:54-55

Mary began her song knowing that she, too, needed a Savior. Next week, we will visit the miraculous birth of Jesus—a beautiful story that fills our hearts with awe and wonder. As joy was shared, remember this: Who we invite into our success matters just as much as those we allow to speak life into our hardest trials.

Zechariah spent the entire pregnancy of his wife in silence. Imagine him simply listening to others, perhaps communicating through tablets. I wonder how much dust his hands collected by the end of that pregnancy. When it was finally time to name the precious baby, they named him John. Once Zechariah confirmed that his son's name would be John, his mouth was opened, and the first thing he did was celebrate with joy and praise!

WEEK 4: DAY 4

God is a God who shows favor. He extends His favor to those who seek Him with pure hearts, desiring to glorify Him through their lives. Zechariah and Elizabeth, who were righteous in the sight of the Lord and longed for a child, served Him not out of obligation but because of their deep love for Him. In doing so, they found favor.

The time was drawing near for the promise of God to unfold—the arrival of the Messiah, the fulfillment of **Genesis 17:6.** The King of Kings was on His way.

Tomorrow, we will close the week by praising alongside Zechariah. God gives us joy because He is filled with joy in order you to 'Count It All Joy!'

You are Crowned in Beauty,

Kimberly

NOTES

WEEK 4: DAY 5

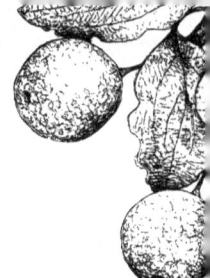

"You Will Be Called"

Zechariah, who had been visited by the Angel Gabriel *(the same angel who visited Mary)*, received a miracle. Favor was extended to him by the miracle-working God. The time Zechariah spent in silence may have been a period of quiet reflection, where he was forced to become a mere observer of this grace. And when his mouth was opened, all that was left was a heart full of praise. This joyful praise, which he offered, was also a prophetic word spoken over his son, John, just as the angel had told him.

Read Luke 1:67-80

My heart overflows with praise, just like Elizabeth's and Zechariah's. So, let's begin today by offering our own praise. Take a moment to praise God for who He is, and write your praise below.

To be known by the Lord for the love in your heart, because of who He is—righteousness itself—fills me with awe. I think back on my life and realize it was God's favor and mercy that saw my heart, and 17 years later, here I am. There was a joy set before me, a joy found in Jesus.

An Unchanging God

What does Luke 1:67-80 reveal about who God is?

WEEK 4: DAY 5

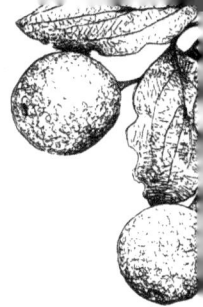

Now, compare Zechariah's song with Hannah's prayer, specifically **1 Samuel 2:1-2** and **6-10**, alongside **Luke 1:67-75**. Use the space to dig deeper.

1 Samuel 2:1-2 & 6-10

"2 Then Hannah prayed and said: "My heart rejoices in the Lord; in the Lord my horn[a] is lifted high. My mouth boasts over my enemies, for I delight in your deliverance. 2 "There is no one holy like the Lord; there is no one besides you; there is no Rock like our God.

6 "The Lord brings death and makes alive; he brings down to the grave and raises up. 7 The Lord sends poverty and wealth; he humbles and he exalts. 8 He raises the poor from the dust and lifts the needy from the ash heap; he seats them with princes and has them inherit a throne of honor. "For the foundations of the earth are the Lord's; on them he has set the world. 9 He will guard the feet of his faithful servants, but the wicked will be silenced in the place of darkness. "It is not by strength that one prevails; 10 those who oppose the Lord will be broken. The Most High will thunder from heaven; the Lord will judge the ends of the earth. "He will give strength to his king and exalt the horn of his anointed."

WEEK 4: DAY 5

Luke 1:67-75

67 His father Zechariah was filled with the Holy Spirit and prophesied: 68 "Praise be to the Lord, the God of Israel, because he has come to his people and redeemed them. 69 He has raised up a horn[a] of salvation for us in the house of his servant David 70 (as he said through his holy prophets of long ago), 71 salvation from our enemies and from the hand of all who hate us— 72 to show mercy to our ancestors and to remember his holy covenant, 73 the oath he swore to our father Abraham: 74 to rescue us from the hand of our enemies, and to enable us to serve him without fear 75 in holiness and righteousness before him all our days. 76 And you, my child, will be called a prophet of the Most High; for you will go on before the Lord to prepare the way for him, 77 to give his people the knowledge of salvation through the forgiveness of their sins, 78 because of the tender mercy of our God,

by which the rising sun will come to us from heaven 79 to shine on those living in darkness

and in the shadow of death, to guide our feet into the path of peace."

80 And the child grew and became strong in spirit[a]; and he lived in the wilderness until he appeared publicly to Israel.

Did you notice that both songs speak of salvation through God's deliverance and that they also exalt the name of the Lord?

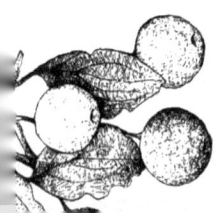

WEEK 4: DAY 5

In **1 Samuel 2:10**, Hannah prophesied that Samuel would be in a place of honor, faithfully serving the Lord. Through Samuel, God would anoint King David, from whose line the 'horn of salvation' would come—Jesus.

According to **Luke 1:69-75**, what does the horn of salvation bring to the people of Israel? (You can place these insights in your treasure chest!)

I imagine that Zechariah lifted up his baby and praised God, as he speaks these powerful words over John.

Read Luke 1:76-79

John would go before the Lord to share this message of unfailing and redeeming love. What a beautiful image! This message would bring restoration through forgiveness, bringing light to dark hearts and a path of peace (v.79).

WEEK 4: DAY 5

The same Holy Spirit who spoke to Abraham, Hannah, Zechariah and Elizabeth is the same one who speaks to your heart today. Regardless of how long it takes, God makes a way for us to be reconciled to Him through the promised child. He would come, live with us, suffer for us, die, and rise from the grave and return for His bride, you and me. Truly, He is our hope. His name is Wonderful Counselor, Mighty God, Everlasting Father, Prince of Peace, as foretold by the prophet Isaiah.

There is joy in the silence. There is joy in the waiting. There is joy in the things in life that don't make sense—because when we look through the eyes of the Source of all joy, Jesus, we come to understand what it means to 'Count it all Joy!'

You are Crowned in Beauty,
Kimberly

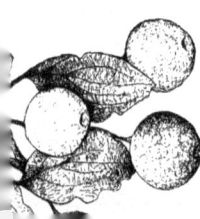

NOTES

NOTES

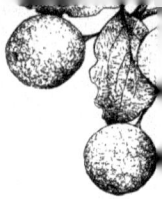

WEEK 5

The Fulfillment of The Promise of Joy!

Mary & Joseph

WEEK 5: DAY 1

The Promise of Joy!

Our faith in action is the evidence of what we truly believe about God, even when it's difficult. It calls us to act and walk out what we believe.

- Abraham obeyed when he was called by God to go to a new nation.
- Hannah faced years of ridicule from Peninnah while believing for a child, and she rose up in faith. She walked into the temple and trusted that God would hear her prayer for a baby.
- Zechariah was serving in the temple when the angel of the Lord appeared to tell him his prayer had been answered.
- Elizabeth was filled with the Holy Spirit when Mary visited her, and she knew she was favored because the mother of her LORD was visiting her.

It all began with faith.

And through faith, we now have the opportunity to accept Jesus as our Lord and Savior. As we grow in our faith, His Word and His life begin to transform us. Through this transformation, we can come to a place of joy, rooted in His love for us. It all started with one man's faith, and today we are adopted into the kingdom of God.

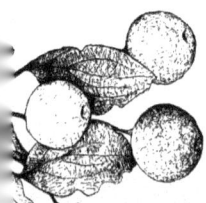

WEEK 5: DAY 1

Reread Genesis 12:1-4

It was all part of God's perfect timing when the angel appeared to Mary, in the town of Nazareth.

Read Luke 1:26-38

Summarize this encounter below.

Read Matthew 1:18-24

How is Joseph a son of David? *(Hint: **Read Matthew 1:1-17**)*

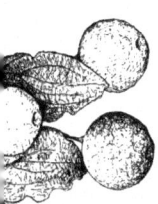

WEEK 5: DAY 1

Read Luke 3:23-38

When we read these verses, we see the beginning of God's redemptive plan for the world through Jesus. This is the beginning of our encounter with joy—joy that will unfold in the coming days and remind us of why Jesus endured pain and suffering for our sake.

There is so much to learn, and the key is to remain teachable. Today's introduction serves as a reminder that God created the heavens and the earth, and He has been with us on this journey to "Count it All Joy!" God has a plan for you as well, and He has given us His written Word as a reliable truth. It's not only something we can depend on, but it is also a powerful sword—through it, we walk in the authority we have in Christ.

I look forward to meeting with you again tomorrow as we explore the lives of two individuals who said, "Yes" to their calling and have played an essential role in your life as well. Now, that's definitely something to 'Count It All Joy' about!

You are Crowned in Beauty,
Kimberly

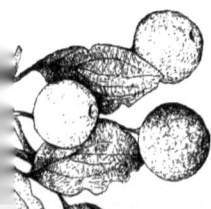

NOTES

WEEK 5: DAY 2

A Place of Honor and Favor

"Hello, you who are highly favored! The Lord is with you!"

(**Luke 1:28** *emphasis mine*)

The favor of the Lord is one that requires humility, obedience, and a righteous heart. It is God who bestows favor on man. As Mary listened to these words from the messenger of God, standing before her, she was troubled. Yet, she was assured that she was favored by God.

In Week 1, we studied the names of God and they continue to appear throughout Scripture. Let's revisit them

Read Luke 1:32-35

Out of all the names that God has, why do you think the Angel of the Lord chose "God Most High" and not another name, such as Sovereign?

God gives us the gift of free will. I believe He chose to remind Mary of His immense power as the Creator of heaven and earth. The child conceived in her womb would be

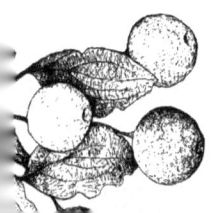

WEEK 5: DAY 2

a miracle, showing how God creates in the unseen. The "Most High" overpowered her for this miracle to take place.

Think back to when Abraham met Melchizedek, the priest in **Genesis 14**, and called God "Most High, Creator of heaven and earth, worthy to be praised, and deliverer." The angel's message to Mary reminds her that she, too, needed a deliverer, as would the people of Israel.

In humility, Mary responds with **Luke 1:38,**

"I am the Lord's servant... May your word to me be fulfilled."

This is miraculous indeed. But we must also consider what it means to be on the other side of someone else's miracle and how it challenges their faith. When Joseph was contemplating divorce, God, in his mercy and grace, sent him an angel in a dream. The Bible tells us that Joseph was considered righteous because he did not want to disgrace Mary publicly.

Read Matthew 1:20-21

WEEK 5: DAY 2

Once again, we read of a deliverer sent to save the world from sin. Joseph obeyed the angel's command.

If you've read these stories before, have they challenged you to look deeper into the way you live out your faith? How are they reaffirming your belief in who God is?

One young woman, facing ridicule from many, and one man, choosing to stay despite the challenges, both walking in obedience and trusting the Lord—this is the example they set for us. Months passed, and the star that led the Magi to the manger finally reached the place where this child was born. We read that the Magi were "overjoyed," and they bowed and worshiped Him. For reference, read **Luke 2:1-12**.

When you look at your life and obedience to God, are there areas where you hesitate to move forward in what He has placed in your heart?

WEEK 5: DAY 2

Read Luke 2:13-23

Joseph and Mary's trials began with God's assurance that there was purpose in what He was calling them to do—both individually and together. The angel of the Lord appeared to them separately, speaking to Joseph in dreams, so that after some time he would act to protect the child and his family.

At the time of Jesus's birth, King Herod was aware of a prophetic word about to be fulfilled. In an attempt to thwart God's plan, he partnered with Satan and ordered the slaughter of all male children under the age of two. But God had other plans.

When we look at Joseph's life, we don't read much about him except for a few key moments: when he and Mary dedicated Jesus at the temple and when their family realized Jesus was missing after they had traveled a day's journey from Jerusalem. Joseph played a crucial role in Jesus's early years. He was a protector, ensuring that the child was kept safe. Joseph understood that the call on his life was worth more than his reputation. He protected Jesus from becoming one of those babies that King Herod sought to destroy.

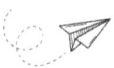

As I reflect on my own life, I realize I blamed the sexual abuse I encountered on my parents and stepfather. I often thought, "If only they had been more aware or present,

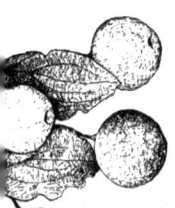

WEEK 5: DAY 2

this wouldn't have happened." Today, I know these were false beliefs, and they played a major role in how I persevered through the pain. At the time, I disassociated myself from the situation, but the enemy sought an opportunity to come in and destroy many things in my life and family—and he ran with it.

Now, about 30 years later, I reflect on the trauma I endured and the deep emotional struggles it caused. I questioned my very existence at times, wondering if I should continue living. Yet, the Lord protected me—even from myself—by providing ways for healing and restoration.

Today, I see His love more clearly than ever. It is a love that is also available to you. His love taught me about forgiveness and how the false beliefs I clung to for years kept me bound to my past. God, in His mercy, sent Jesus to suffer for all of us.

To live a life of joy begins when we reflect on the state of our hearts.
Are we living righteously? Are we living honorably? Are you an example of Joy?

Would you consider your own life as an example of joy—despite the trials and the hurt you've faced? Is it worth holding on to what was, or what someone did to you in the past?

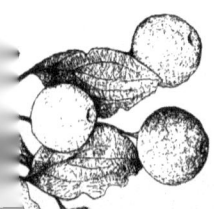

WEEK 5: DAY 2

I want to be counted as righteous and highly favored, and that is a privilege. I want the same for you, friend. This is why I am here with you—learning alongside you that a life in Christ is worth 'Counting It All Joy,' even in the midst of trials.

You are deeply loved,

Kimberly

NOTES

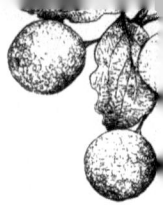

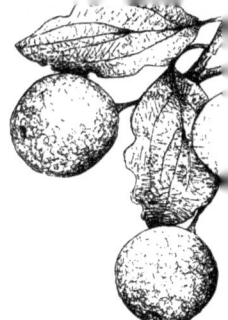

WEEK 5: DAY 3

The Promise of Joy

In the beginning, the Most High, El Elyon, had a plan. He knew the end from the start, and blessed are we to have it written down, so that we can invite Him into our lives to rule and reign. That invitation was made possible through Jesus Christ, God's only Son.

He humbled himself and made his life a living sacrifice for the forgiveness of our sins. He came humbly as a baby, and his birth had been awaited for centuries. It was prophesied by many, and spoken of to Abraham, by El Elyon Himself.

As we've looked closely at the lives of Abraham and Sarah, Hannah and Elkanah, Elizabeth and Zechariah, and Mary and Joseph, we see lives that surrendered themselves to God for a bigger purposes. Leading to the birth of Jesus, is there a common thread interwoven through each of their lives?

Abraham → Hannah → Elizabeth → Mary & Joseph → Jesus

The stories within the Bible are full of tragedy, triumph, wisdom, sorrow, and purpose. Each one came to a surrender.

Their lives all played a major role in ushering the coming of the promised child. When we read these stories, it's easy to forget the trials these people faced. There are stories of those who rose to positions of authority and influence, people who escaped their enemies, and others who hid in caves because their lives were in

WEEK 5: DAY 3

danger—like King David. Some prophets were warned of devastation and destruction, sharing visions of the holy temple and God's redemptive plan for His chosen people, Israel.

All of these stories led to one man: Jesus.

Jesus lived a life of service. He modeled God's love and only did what the Father told Him to do **(John 5:19)**. The Gospels share the life and ministry of Jesus. If you are new to the faith, I encourage you to read the Book of John in its entirety. That was where I began in 2008 when I gave my life to Jesus as Lord and Savior.

Before we begin today's reflection, let's set our hearts to receive new insight and wisdom from God. Take a moment to pray and thank our loving and gracious Father for the life of Jesus.

Read John 1:1-14

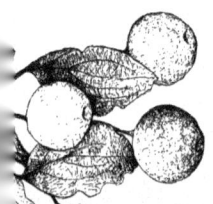

WEEK 5: DAY 3

Who was in the beginning, and what was in Him? When you read verses 10-11, think about who in your life could benefit from hearing the testimony of your faith and what Jesus has done for you. Pray about it and consider sharing it with them.

Read John 1:19-27 & 29-40

Reread verses 29-31 and write down the tone of voice you hear in your mind when reading them. What is the feeling you experience as you read John's words?

Whenever I read these verses, certain words jump out at me, and I am filled with peace and joy. Because of the Spirit of God that filled John when Mary visited Elizabeth, I recognize that it was the same Spirit that rested upon Jesus. The Lord showed John the Spirit that was resting on Jesus, and that is the same Spirit of prophecy that testifies about Jesus Christ **(Revelation 19:10)**.

John certainly prepared the way for Jesus and the kingdom of God, even if it meant correcting people and ultimately losing his life, as we read in **Matthew 14:1-12** and

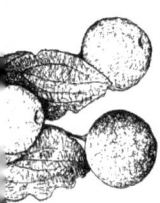

WEEK 5: DAY 3

Luke 9:7-9. John's life was a testimony of pure service to the Lord, preparing people to receive the Messiah. Jesus had to become greater, and John had to become less. His life was an act of joy in doing so.

When you think about the joy that John exemplified, does it encourage you about your purpose and role in furthering the kingdom of God? Is Christ becoming greater than your circumstances in life?

I know it's not always easy. I've had moments when I wanted to hide like Jonah under a plant and just perish because my eyes were focused on the negatives I saw. There have been valleys so dark that I couldn't see how I would ever get out, weighed down by oppression. Mentally, I reached a place of agony and desperation. It's hard to put yourself out there and be vulnerable, especially as I write this.

My prayer is that on these pages, you will be reminded of just how precious you are to God. After the birth of my son, I faced one of the biggest trials of my life. Today, I'm on the other side of it, and still learning to choose joy on days where I am reminded of the pain. Those three years were joy-less. Yes, you read that right—I couldn't see joy. I know joy is meant to be a constant state of contentment, especially in living for Jesus. I know this, and some of us do. But the suffering in my

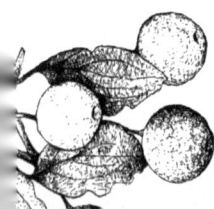

WEEK 5: DAY 3

heart was so heavy that it was only by the grace of God that I had the courage to face this turmoil, on my knees, fully surrendering day by day. Sometimes in our suffering we forget that the suffering of Christ was filled with joy, because of his love for us. Before we close today, think about one of your greatest sufferings and write it down below. Share how you felt, who was there to pray you through and where God was in all of it.

In my suffering I knew God was there holding me each day. As much as I do not want to admit this, the suffering of this time in my heart which I will share about more tomorrow became an idol. It was easier for me to run to crying and living sorrow-filled while at the same time declaring joy, declaring restoration of my heart, body and mind.

I am thankful for the examples of those who went before us, reminding me, and I hope reminding you too, to 'Count It All Joy.'

You are Crowned in Beauty,

Kimberly

NOTES

WEEK 5: DAY 4

The Joy in the Waiting

There is joy in the waiting and in the suffering. Though it may be hidden for a time, when the light shines and our thoughts are purified by God's Word, joy radiates.

Today, we embark on one final quest to dig up treasures in the stories of the life and ministry of Jesus. I challenge you to reflect on **Hebrews 12:2,** which says that, "The joy set before him" was what motivated Jesus on the cross.

As you read through the stories below, search for clues about Jesus' purpose. Write down at least three words that summarize them and explain why you chose these words.

Read the following verses.

- John 4:1-26, 39-42
- John 9:1-12
- John 10:1-18
- John 11:1-16, 38-43

WEEK 5: DAY 4

The woman at the well, the man at the pool of Bethesda, the blind man, the story of the Good Shepherd, and the death and resurrection of Lazarus are just a few examples of how Jesus extended grace and love through miracles. These accounts reveal a servant who embodied God's love and mission. Through Jesus, we learn that we have a Shepherd who leads us, teaches us how to live in freedom and forgiveness, and calls us to have eyes of compassion that glorify God. These are lives that show us power and authority—the same power and authority that Jesus had.

Ultimately, we are given to share in the power and authority through Jesus, but always with the aim of glorifying God.

There is an exchange that happens through Jesus. Much like the covenant of circumcision in Abraham's time, Jesus made a physical exchange at the cross through His blood.

He was betrayed by one of His own disciples, Judas Iscariot, for money.
He was forgotten by others, with Peter denying Him.
He was beaten beyond recognition, mocked, spat on, and crowned with thorns.

Jesus exchanged His life for the betrayals, denials, pride, offenses, and hate that were heaped upon Him. He endured this all, though he could have called down legions of angels to save him. He chose to stay on the cross for us all.

I remember standing in a 900-year-old chapel in Leicester, feeling nothing but numbness. My husband and I decided to move forward with our final embryo transfer.

WEEK 5: DAY 4

At almost 11 weeks we lost her. With it, my joy seemed to vanish. Months passed, and I was still dealing with physical complications. My mind and spirit tried to hold on to hope, especially for the baby boy I already had, but my heart wept. In that chapel, I cried out to the Lord, asking, "Why did you allow this to happen, especially after everything I've been through in my life?"

In that moment, I felt the Lord fill my heart with these words: "I needed you to understand how I value life. Man tries to make life, some take life, but I will always be the Giver of life."

A sense of peace washed over me, and tears streamed down my cheeks. I realized that no matter what happened in life, God was always, and would always be, the Giver of life. I had no control over life, but I could build my faith in that moment—and that's what I chose to do.

The loss of that pregnancy triggered past traumas, reminding me of deep pain and violations I had long buried. It was only through the grace of God that I was able to face this deep sorrow. On my knees, fully surrendering day by day.

Repentance Leads to Reconciliation

For much of my Christian life, I carried deeply rooted offenses—many of which had been with me for years. But God is merciful and faithful. He never leaves us, even through our trials.

WEEK 5: DAY 4

Read Luke 23:34

"Father, forgive them, for they do not know what they are doing"
Why was Jesus saying these words out loud and to God?

Do you think those witnessing this moment understood the power of his prayer?

This is a pivotal moment for me, and I believe it is for you too. I've been vulnerable with you, and now I ask you to be vulnerable with God.

The offenses I held onto through much of my life kept my joy conditional—based on the people around me and the outcomes I expected. I placed my joy in circumstances and achievements, not realizing that these deeply rooted hurts were tied to false beliefs. My past decisions, including the trauma and choices I made, had led to these beliefs. And so, I began to repent.

When you think about Jesus on the cross, saying, "Father, forgive them, for they do not know what they are doing," does that stir your heart to forgive?
What if those people don't know Jesus?
Do you still feel called to forgive them?

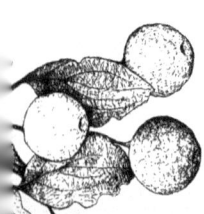

WEEK 5: DAY 4

Un-forgiveness and offense are heavy burdens. God knows this, and He calls us to forgive.

Where in your life are you holding on to un-forgiveness or offense?
Are you brave enough to lay it down at the foot of the cross and never pick it up again?
Write it down.

God is a forgiving God. He sent Jesus to die on the cross so that we could have eternal life. Jesus took all of our pain, every single inch of it. Our reconciliation with Christ is a daily surrender. Tomorrow, we will continue on this journey, remembering that our calling is to Count It All Joy—even in the midst of trials. He loves you dearly.

You are Crowned in Beauty,
Kimberly

NOTES

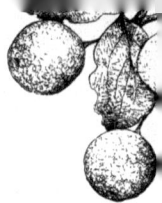

WEEK 5: DAY 5

Count It All Joy!

I am so proud of you, friend. We've made it to the last day of this treasure hunt, and there are countless treasures awaiting you every day of your life.

God is so faithful, and His love is unfailing. He gave us this gift.

Each day, we can choose to be more like Jesus and count everything as joy!

As we confessed our offenses yesterday, today we will focus on a life of continuous reconciliation.

Read John 15:1-17

God prunes things, people, and habits from our lives when they no longer keep us connected to Him. Perhaps there are things in your life that hinder your ability to be joyful. Whatever is keeping you from living a life of peace and joy, you must remain in Him at all cost.

I realize that with time, commitment, and the guidance of an anointed woman of God—my counselor Brenda—I began to see that the root of my offenses lay in believing lies about who I believed I was. These lies caused me to think that I deserved the pain and trauma I experienced earlier in my life. I know many can relate to this, and my heart is truly saddened by it.

WEEK 5: DAY 5

No one deserves to be defiled, betrayed, abused, or ridiculed. What I didn't understand at the time was that, through these false beliefs, I was offending God. When we are made into a new creation, the old is gone, and the new has come. Jesus wiped away all my sins—and the sins of those who hurt me. I had been living a life where I appeared to be fine on the outside, but deep inside, I didn't truly believe what God said about me, which in turns offends him.

Read Isaiah 61:1-11

God gives us a "crown of beauty for ashes,
Oil of joy for mourning,
A garment of praise for despair."

Read 2 Corinthians 7:10

The cleansing that comes through confession draws us closer to God. Repentance is necessary because we are made in His image. Anything that keeps us from Him or leads us to believe things that contradict His word must be dealt with.

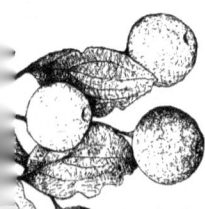

WEEK 5: DAY 5

On that day in the 900-year-old chapel in Leicester, after God spoke to my heart, He led me to meditate on the power of the blood of Jesus on the cross. Months and years passed, and one day, during a counseling session, I confessed my hatred toward my abuser. I realized that there was no way I could approach the throne of grace and receive forgiveness for my sins if I hadn't forgiven him. So, I did it wholeheartedly. I forgave him, and I forgave myself for many things, especially for offending God with my prideful heart, because I did not want to show weakness. I also forgave myself for not allowing the Lord to minister to my heart and for getting in His way by thinking I had all the answers.

He cuts off every branch…

I blamed myself for the loss of our baby, for the abuse, for my father's absence, and for falling into the occult. These were all false beliefs. Yes, certain things contributed to those situations, but it was truly how I saw myself—unworthy of love—that kept me in bondage. I had to confess that I felt unworthy of God's love.

If you remain in me…

To remain means to abide, to let go, and never leave-(in Hebrew) Harpu. Jesus gave His life with joy as He faithfully served with purpose—to give us eternal life through the

WEEK 5: DAY 5

the forgiveness of our sins. When the first drop of His blood fell on the earth, it marked the beginning of our reconciliation with God. That first drop of blood redeemed us and bought us back.

On my own, there is nothing I can do to win God's love. It's not a competition—it's only grace, undeserved grace. Today, I see that God sees me, and I live to serve Him and honor Him each day —not to offend Him and to do everything with joy.

Read Hebrews 12:1-3

Consider Him in your trials.

Consider Him on the cross.

He endured all of this so that you could persevere in this life and be made complete in Him. For the joy of the promise of eternal life was made through Him. He took your trials, your sin, and your offenses upon the cross. He loves you dearly, friend. He tells us to "cast our cares upon Him, to call on Him, abide in Him, rejoice, and be made holy in Him." Dig up the truth and speak it over yourself. Let others disciple you in the faith!

Search for five verses that speak about joy and write them in the spaces below. I've got the first for you!

- Galatians 5:22- But the fruit of the Spirit is love, joy, peace, forbearance, kindness, goodness, faithfulness

WEEK 5: DAY 5

Our Last Treasure Awaits

James, a servant of God and of the Lord Jesus Christ, wrote:
"Consider it pure joy when you face trials of many kinds because you know that the testing of your faith produces perseverance. Let perseverance finish its work so that you may be complete, not lacking anything. And if any of you lack wisdom, let him ask of God, who gives generously to all without finding fault..." **(James 1:2-5)**

"Blessed is the one who perseveres under trial because, having stood the test, that person will receive the crown of life that the Lord has promised to those who love Him." **James 1:12**

You and I know that we love Him. So, friend, because we love Him, live a life of seeking His heart and His desires for your life in every situation. James tells us that we will be tested throughout our lives. These trials will ground us in our faith, and when we need help—wisdom, understanding, or guidance—all we need to do is ask God.

Continue to 'find beauty in the ashes of every day life' and "Count It All Joy!" because you *are* Crowned in Beauty and you wear it well!
Remember, He will bring people along your journey to sharpen you,
so that you can receive the Crown of Life!

Your Sister In Christ,
Kimberly

NOTES

NOTES

NOTES

NOTES

TREASURE CHEST

COUNT ALL THE TREASURES *joy*

TREASURE CHEST

COUNT ALL THE TREASURES OF TRIALS *joy*

NAMES OF GOD

COUNT ALL THE TREASURES

El Elyon- God Most High

El Shaddai- The Sovereign God, All-Sufficient

El Roi- The God Who Sees

El Olam- The Everlasting God

Jehovah Jireh- The Lord will Provide

YHYW- I AM, I AM who I AM

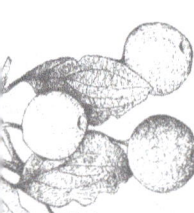

BIBLE VERSES

WEEK 1

Genesis 3:8-10, James 1:1-5, 12, John 15:2, Genesis 14:14-20, Genesis 14, John 1:1-5, Genesis 15:2-8, Genesis 16, Genesis 17:1, Psalm 119:41, 2 Peter 3:8-9, Matthew 6:33, Romans 8:13, Isaiah 53, Numbers 23:19, Joshua 23:10, Psalm 119:41, Psalm 119:50, Psalm 119:57-58, 2 Samuel 7:25-26, Isaiah 6:8, Philippians 2:3, 1 Corinthians 10:24, Isaiah 54:10

WEEK 2

Genesis 12, Genesis 11:26-32, Genesis 8:20-9:17, Genesis 3:20, Leviticus 17:11, Romans 12:1, Matthew 6:33, James 1:25, Philippians 4:8, Genesis 12:2-3,7, 10-12, Genesis 13:5-11, 14-17, Genesis 14:1-16, Genesis 15:12-16, Genesis 16, Genesis 17, Genesis 18, Genesis 20, 2 Peter 3:9, Genesis 21:1-6,8-20, Genesis 19:26, Genesis 22:8, Genesis 22:12-16, James 1:5,

WEEK 3

Romans 2:11, 1 Samuel 1:1-7, 1 Samuel 1:6-11, Exodus 3, Psalm 34:6, Psalm 28:7, 1 Samuel 1:14, 1 Samuel 2, 1 Samuel 1:15–16, Proverbs 18:21, 1 Samuel 1:21-22, Deuteronomy 23:23, 1 John 4:13-18, 1 Samuel 1:23-26, 1 Samuel 2:8-10, 1 Samuel 1:23, 1 Samuel 1:18-21, 1 Samuel 1:27-28, Jeremiah 1:5,

WEEK 4

2 Peter 3:8, Luke 1:1-7, 2 Corinthians 5:17, Luke 1:11-17, Genesis 15, Luke 1:18–20, Luke 1:23-24, Luke 1:26-38, Luke 1:39-45, Luke 1:54-55, Genesis 17:6, Luke 1:67-80, Luke 1:67-80, 1 Samuel 1:1-2, 6-10, Luke 1:67-75, 1 Samuel 1:66, Luke 1:76-79,

WEEK 5

Genesis 12:1-4, Luke 1:26-38, Matthew 1:18-24, Matthew 1:1-17, Luke 3:23-38, Luke 1:28, Luke 1:32-35, Genesis 14, Luke 1:38, Matthew 1:20-21, Luke 2:1-12, Luke 2:13-23, John 5:19, John 1:1-14, John 1:19-27, 29-40, Revelation 19:10, Matthew 14:1-12, Luke 9:7-9, Hebrews 12:2, John 4:1-26, 39-42, John 9:1-12, John 10:1-18, John 11:1-16, 38-43, Luke 23:34, John 15:1-17, Isaiah 61:1-11, Galatians 5:22, Hebrews 12:1-3, James 1:2-5, 12, 2 Corinthians 7:10

ENDNOTES

NIV First-Century Study Bible, Zonadervan, ©2014
with Endnotes by Kent Dobson

Commentaries used from https://biblehub.com and NIV First-Century Study Bible, onadervan, ©2014
with Endnotes by Kent Dobson

Character
https://www.merriam-webster.com/dictionary/character

Perseverance
https://www.merriam-webster.com/dictionary/perseverance

Sovereign
https://www.merriam-webster.com/dictionary/sovereign

In-Vitro Fertilization
https://www.mayoclinic.org/tests-procedures/in-vitro-fertilization/about/pac-20384716

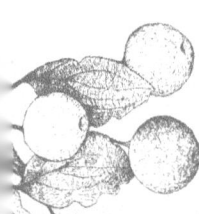

ABOUT THE MINISTRY

FINDING BEAUTY IN THE ASHES OF EVERY DAY LIFE.
ISAIAH 61:3

OUR MISSION

To see a generation of women rise from brokenness into beauty—women who live unoffended, surrender wholly to God, and radiate His love, wisdom, and power in every sphere of influence.

OUR VALUES

TO PARTNER WITH US
VISIT US AT WWW.CROWNEDINBEAUTY.COM

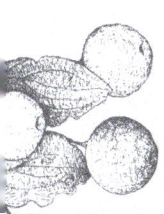

BOOKS

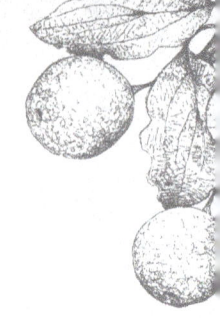

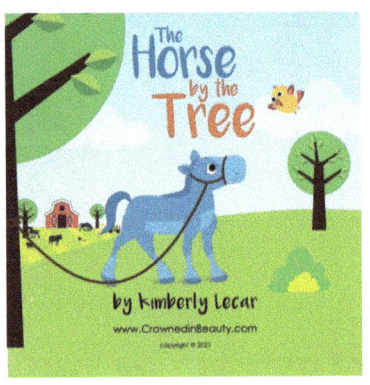

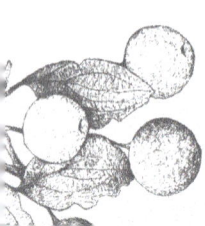

VISIT OUR BOOK SHOP AT
WWW.CROWNEDINBEAUTY.COM/SHOP

Fountain of Hope Counseling

Fountain of Hope Counseling

Our mission is to instill hope and promote personal healing and mental health wellness through counseling for children and adults.

Brenda Parker MSC, LPC

Brenda received a Bachelor of Science in Nursing from Missouri Western State University and a Master's in Mental Health Counseling from University of Phoenix. Brenda is the founder of Fountain of Hope Counseling, Inc, a 501(c)3 nonprofit organization and is a Licensed Professional Counselor. Brenda has extensive experience as a forensic interviewer working with law enforcement, County Attorney's Office and Department of Child Safety in multiple counties. Brenda has been providing mental health counseling to children, adolescents and adults with a diverse range of presenting concerns in the behavioral health field while developing her dream as an independent therapist.

Brenda's passion and interests lie in providing empathic, genuine, strength-based counseling for mental health concerns including grief counseling, loss of self-worth, depression, anxiety, adjustment disorders with various mixed emotions, and sexual trauma. Brenda uses an eclectic approach to providing mental health counseling or therapy through faith-based counseling, existentialism, TF CBT, Gestalt's empty chair technique, Person-Centered approach, motivational interviewing and education. Brenda provides counseling services for children using parallel play techniques and mindfulness games with adolescents.

Phone 520-266-1819
brenda@fountainofhopecounseling.org
fountainofhopecounseling.org

www.ingramcontent.com/pod-product-compliance
Lightning Source LLC
Chambersburg PA
CBHW080413170426
43194CB00015B/2793